99 FUN-TO-MAKE ELECTRONICS PROJECTS

BY CY TYMONY

TAB BOOKS Inc.

BLUE RIDGE SUMMIT, PA. 17214

FIRST EDITION

THIRD PRINTING

Printed in the United States of America

Reproduction or publication of the content in any manner, without express
permission of the publisher, is prohibited. No liability is assumed with respect to
the use of the information herein.

Library of Congress Cataloging in Publication Data

Cy Tymony
    99 fun-to-make electronics projects.

    Includes index.
    1. Electronics—Amateur's manuals.   I. Title.
II. Title: Ninety-nine fun-to-make electronics projects.
TK9965.T93   621.3815   81-9098
ISBN 0-8306-0002-7   AACR2
ISBN 0-8306-1288-2 (pbk.)

Contents

Preface

Electronics parts miniaturization has spawned many new products during the last few years such as, multi-function watches, computers for the home and hand-held electronic games. Manufacturers are receiving good returns on their investments in electronic parts by selling ready-made products using LEDs which blink on and off.

You, the inventive electronics hobbyist, can go a step further and build your own LED projects. Only you, not a mass market manufacturer, know what gadgets you and your friends can put to use.

I've received much praise and admiration from people who I've made LED gifts for. I believe you will, too. Let's get started.

Cy Tymony

Dedication

This book is dedicated to Cloise Shaw, Keven Burnley, Bob Collins and Anthony R. Curtis. It would not have been possible without their assistance and understanding.

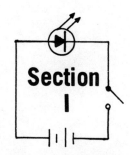

Section
I

Making Electronic Gifts

Section I
Making Electronic Gifts

This section should be read carefully before any of the projects are constructed. Making electronic gifts is a new art/trade and different techniques are used for every gift produced. Here are a few tips I'm sure will make your gift constructing time easier and give your projects a professional appearance.

Construct circuits on a thin piece of cardboard. Mount the components as close together as possible and lay them flat for a thin streamlined appearance (and to fit into small spaces). IC pins must be bent straight out and connected to other components with very thin diameter connecting wire (insulated of course). Use the smallest and thinnest watch batteries you can find for portable power supplies.

Whenever possible, use flat rectangular LEDs for projects that use them. Place a small piece of plastic mirror paper under the LED to reflect more light. Cover LEDs with material cloth, dark translucent plastic or plastic mirror paper. This gives them an invisible "blacked out" look when they are not on.

And most importantly, become more aesthetic. That is, listen to what people say about their preferences of color, taste and style. Find out as much as you can about their needs and desires. Visit gift shops and clothing stores. Pay attention to how they package and present their merchandise. All of the aforementioned footwork will help you design and build a more personalized gift for that special person. It only takes a few cents more to buy a decorative gift box, a couple of stick-on initials, a gift card and a rose (when applicable) but believe me, it will make a tremendous difference to your gift's new owner!

CIRCUITS

Basically, there are two types of circuits: series and parallel. A series circuit is one in which all of the devices are wired "hand to hand". See Fig. I-1. In this circuit the devices are dependent upon one another. If one LED goes out, they all go out. The word circuit means, "a going around", and that is how electricity flows, in a circular pattern.

A parallel circuit is one that allows the components to draw power from the battery independently of each other. In this manner, if one component (such as a LED) is inoperative, the other components can continue functioning. See Fig. I-2.

SWITCHES

Switches are used to control the operation of a device by allowing electrical power to flow through them. There will be two different types of switches used in this book: open and closed. An open switch is one that is in the "off" position until depressed. A closed switch is one that is in the "on" position until depressed. See Fig. I-3 for a push-button switch. See Fig. I-4 for a normally open (NO) switch, and a normally closed (NC) switch.

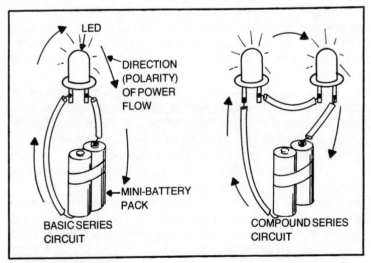

Fig. I-1. The series circuit.

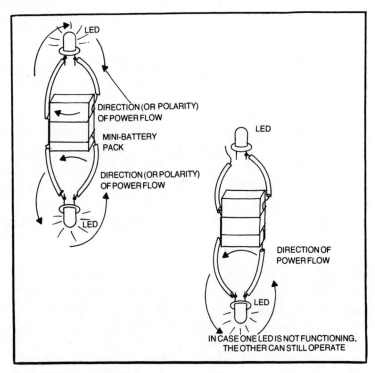

Fig. I-2. The parallel circuit.

LEAD WIRE

Lead wire is used to connect components and devices together; i.e., LEDs to battery packs. Always use insulated wire so the circuits will be protected when put in close quarters. See Figs. I-5 and I-6. Be sure to check that the lead wire is always connected firmly to each device.

Fig. I-3. A push-button switch.

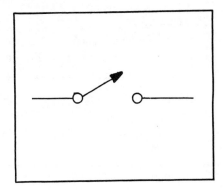

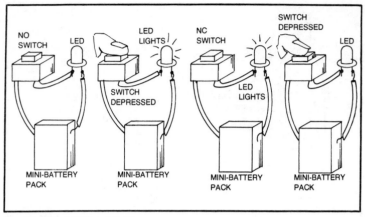

Fig. I-4. NO and NC switches.

BATTERIES

There will be two kinds of *battery packs* referred to in this book. The first is called simply, *a battery pack*. It consists of two AA batteries in a holder and a 9 volt battery clip attached. See Fig. I-7. Some projects will also use a regular 9 volt battery.

The second kind of battery used will be the thin watch or calculator type battery. These will be taped together with wire leads and called "*a mini-battery pack*". See Fig. I-8.

RESISTORS

Resistors are devices used to limit current and/or voltage going to a component. They are calibrated in *ohms* (100 ohms, 500 ohms, etc.). Incidentally, 1k ohms means 1,000 ohms and 1 meg ohms means 1,000,000 ohms. Their resistance is measured by (or represented by) the color bands on the resistor. See Fig. I-9.

SOLAR CELLS

Solar cells are small flat square devices that convert light energy into electrical energy. They can be used to power leds if

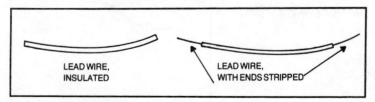

Fig. I-5. Insulated lead wire.

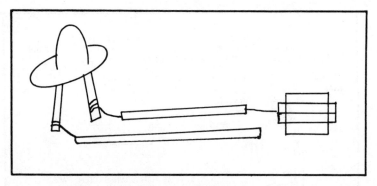

Fig. I-6. Using lead wire to connect a battery to a LED.

enough of them are wired in series and there is ample light from the sun, an incandescent light or a flourescent light. Like a battery, they have positive and negative lead wires. If your device will be exposed to light when in use, you might want to substitute solar cells for regular batteries for a more permanent power supply. See Figs. I-10 and I-11.

LEDS

A LED is a light emitting diode. A diode is a device that lets electricity pass through it in only one direction. A light emitting diode glows like a small light while electricity is passing through it. If you connect it in the wrong way, it will not light. See Figs. I-12 through I-15.

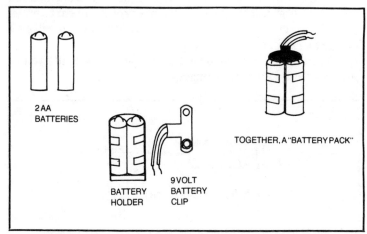

Fig. I-7. A battery pack.

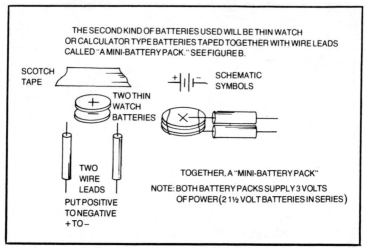

Fig. I-8. A mini-battery pack.

Flashing LEDs

A flashing LED is a device that is basically a LED with a tiny integrated circuit (IC) inside it, that makes it flash on and off when it is connected to a battery. It must be connected in the right direction (polarity) to light. See Figs. I-16 through I-17.

Tri-Colored LEDs

A tri-colored LED is a device with two LEDs combined into one. The LEDs are connected in reverse polarity (direction), if you connect at least 1.75 volts to it in one direction it will emit a green glow. If you reverse the polarity of the electrical power, it will emit orange (or red). See Figs. I-18 and I-19.

These LEDs are called tri-color because they emit a yellow light when used with alternating current.

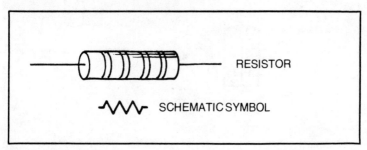

Fig. I-9. A resistor.

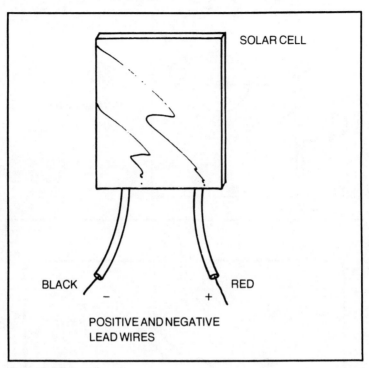

Fig. I-10. A solar cell.

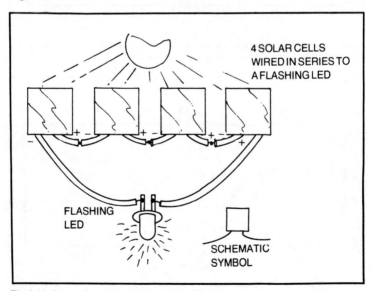

Fig. I-11. Four solar cells in series with a LED.

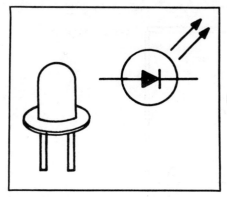

Fig. I-12. A light emitting diode.

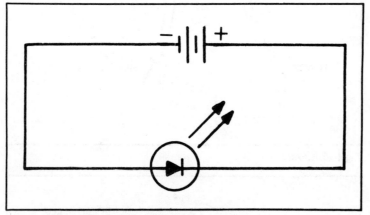

Fig. I-13. LED connected in wrong direction (or polarity).

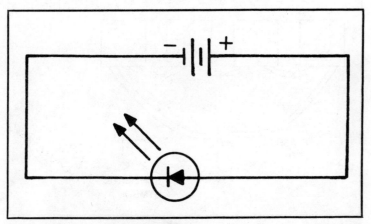

Fig. I-14. LED connected in proper direction.

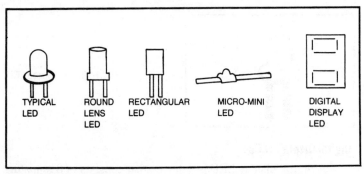

Fig. I-15. Various LEDs.

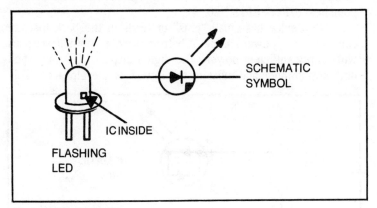

Fig. I-16. A flashing LED.

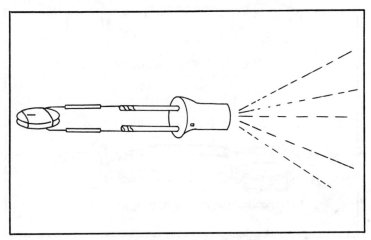

Fig. I-17. A flashing LED connected to a mini-battery pack.

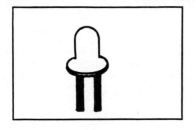

Fig. I-18. Tri-colored LED.

Digital Display LEDs

A digital display LED is a device that consists of 8 miniature LEDs that are positioned in the form of a number 8 with a decimal point next to it. See Fig. I-20.

The device has small "pins" or leads in the back that are connected to a power source. A battery pack or mini-battery pack will supply sufficient power. The digital display LED can "spell out" any number and most of the letters of the alphabet. This

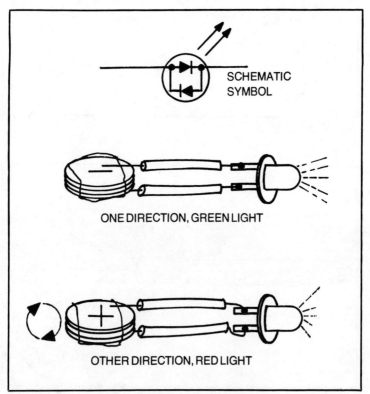

SCHEMATIC SYMBOL

ONE DIRECTION, GREEN LIGHT

OTHER DIRECTION, RED LIGHT

Fig. I-19. Tri-colored LEDs emit two different colors using DC.

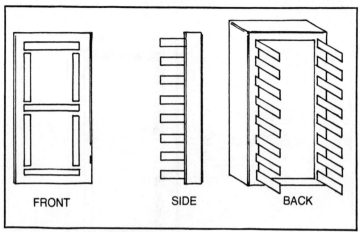

Fig. I-20. Seven segment LED with decimal point.

device is commonly used in electronic watches, calculators and electronic games. See Fig. I-21.

The device will have a common negative lead (–) or ground, so you can connect your battery pack's negative lead to this wire and the positive wire to the lead of the segment you want to light on the LED. See Fig. I-22.

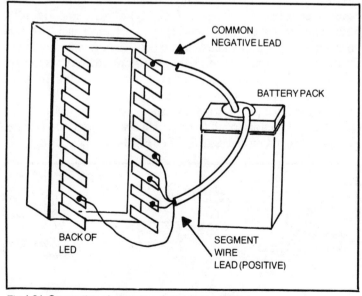

Fig. I-21. Connecting a battery to a digital display LED.

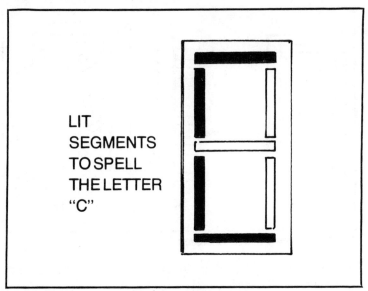

LIT
SEGMENTS
TO SPELL
THE LETTER
"C"

Fig. I-22. Locating the negative or ground pin.

MINI-LAMPS

Mini-lamps are small incandescent lights similar to the ones used in room or office lamps, only smaller. They can be wired to a battery pack in either direction (polarity) to light. See Fig. I-23. The advantages of using mini-lamps is their small size and brightness. It is preferable that you use 1½ or 3 volt mini-lamps with projects in this book since they are powered by a 3 volt power source (battery packs). Keep in mind that the 1½ volt mini-lamps will light brighter than the 3 volt lamps, (when wired to a 3 volt battery pack) but they will not last as long. However, you can wire two-1½ volt mini-lamps in *series* with a 3 volt battery pack to get the same brightness and lamp life. See Fig. I-24.

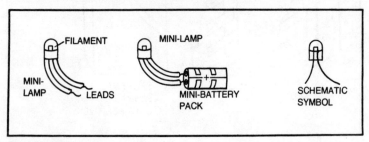

Fig. I-23. A mini-lamp.

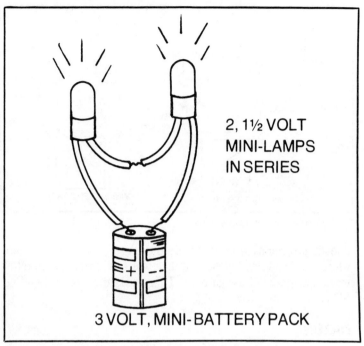

Fig. I-24. Two 1½ volt Mini-lamps in series with a 3 volt supply.

POTENTIOMETERS (POTS)

A *pot* is a variable resistor, a device that can limit and vary the amount of electrical power going to a device such as a LED. When wired in series with a device and its power supply, a pot can control the brightness of a LED, the flash rate of a flashing LED or the loudness of a buzzer. See Fig. I-25.

MERCURY SWITCHES

A mercury switch is a device which will open or close a circuit depending upon its physical position. It is basically a small container with 2 leads inside. The container holds a small drop of mercury which can move around and depending upon the mercury switch's position, can complete the circuit between the two leads. See Fig. I-26.

REED SWITCHES

A reed switch is a device which closes a circuit when in the presence of a magnetic field. It is a little glass (or plastic) tube with

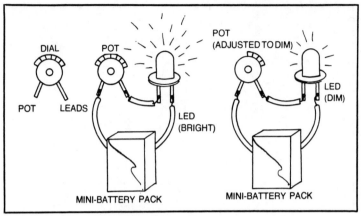

Fig. I-25. How a potentiometer works.

2 leads protruding from it. Inside there are two pieces of metal which are positioned close together which will touch each other when a magnet is brought near. This closes the circuit. See Fig. I-27.

BUZZERS

Buzzers used in this book for audible purposes can be found in most hardware or electronic stores. It is preferable to use small,

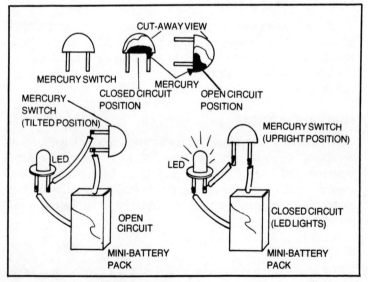

Fig. I-26. The mercury switch and how it works.

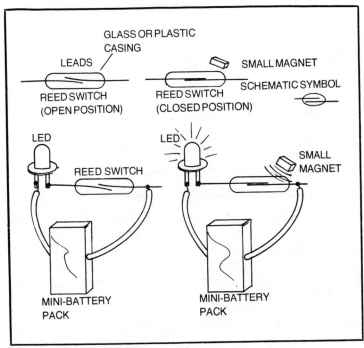

Fig. I-27. The reed switch and how it works.

lightweight buzzers that operate on a 3 volt power supply. Buzzers usually draw a lot of electrical power quickly so it is advisable to use them sparingly with projects. See Figs. I-28 and I-29. You will be able to find buzzers with various tones, with very to deep light chirping sounds.

ELECTRIC MOTORS

You can find small electric motors, for some of the projects in this book, at most electronics parts stores. Obtain motors that are low speed and that operate on 1½ to 3 volts. You can simply attach the motor's leads to a battery pack and it will run (polarity will decide which direction it will spin). See Figs. I-30 and I-31.

FLASHER ICS WITH CAPACITORS

A *flasher IC* (integrated circuit) is a small device that can make LED flash on and off. It does this by the use of the miniature electronic components inside it such as transistors and resistors. It only needs a capacitor (300 μf) to make it flash. A capacitor is an electronic component that can store small amounts of electricity

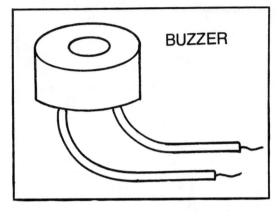

BUZZER

Fig. I-28. A buzzer.

and release the electricity later. The projects that use the flasher IC in this book will all be connected in the same way. The flasher IC can be found at most electronic parts stores under its designated part number, LM3909. Its package/instructions will give more details of its operation in addition to other ways to make it perform in electronic circuits. See Figs. I-32 and I-33.

SPECIAL FLASHING DEVICES

You can make LEDs flash on and off using transistor circuits or IC timers but the simplest way is to wire and LED in series with a flasher LED. The flasher LED has a small IC inside it that makes it flash and it will also make another LED or string of LEDs that are in series with it flash on and off. Be sure to allow only about 2 volts per LED included in this series circuit because too much voltage will cause the flasher LED to turn off. It will also eventually damage the flasher LED permanently.

Flasher LEDs will increase their flash rate in response to light shining on them. If you position them in a place where the light will change intensity, it will flash the LEDs wired in series faster and slower producing an interesting effect. You'll notice that throughout this book LEDs are made to flash using either the flasher LED, the flasher IC or you can also use the 555 timer IC. Each device gives its own varied flashing effect. See Fig. I-34.

The flasher LED keeps the LEDs, that are in series with it, *on* and then turns them *off* suddenly. It is very compact and can double for part of the light effect itself.

The flasher IC keeps the LEDs in the off state and then flashes them suddenly giving a mysterious effect. It also uses power stored in the capacitor to produce the sudden flash so it is very

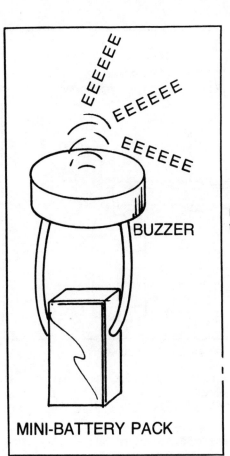

EEEEE EEEEEE EEEEEE

BUZZER

MINI-BATTERY PACK

Fig. I-29. A buzzer connected to a mini-battery pack.

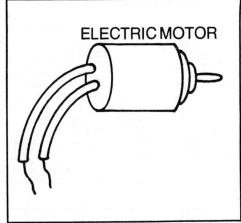

ELECTRIC MOTOR

Fig. I-30. A small electric motor.

25

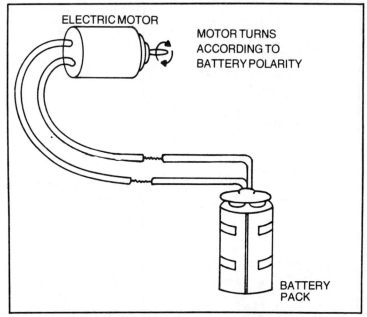

Fig. I-31. Small electric motor connected to a battery pack.

efficient in using power. In fact, the flasher IC can turn on an LED even when the power supply is as low as 1.2 volts! It will flash an LED continuously for a full year if used with a single C cell, 1½ volt battery.

The 555 timer IC can also be used to flash LEDs but because it needs at least 5 volts of power and three extra components (resistors and capacitors) I only use it in projects as a clock pulse

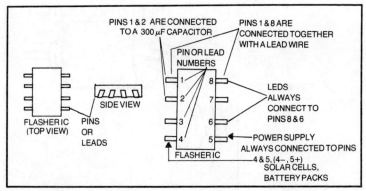

Fig. I-32. LM3909 flasher IC.

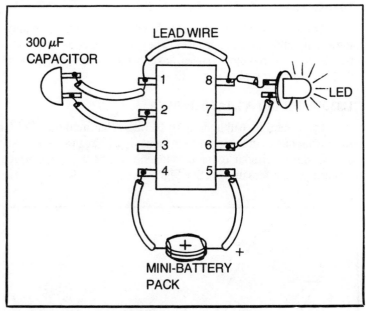

Fig. I-33. Typical flasher IC circuit.

for the 4017 decade counter IC. But don't let this stop you from using this super versatile device for your own circuit designs.

Important Note: When wiring digital LEDs to spell out a name and using the 4017 decade counter IC to flash each letter, use diodes going to each digital LED segment. This will prevent segments lighting up when they aren't supposed to.

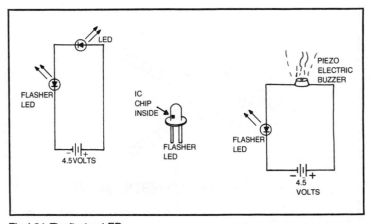

Fig. I-34. The flasher LED.

TRANSISTORS

Transistors are devices used for switching current, amplifying a signal and for other purposes. They will be used as switches in this book. The projects that use transistors need only NPN general purpose transistors. See Fig. I-35.

LM3914 BAR/DOT DISPLAY DRIVER

This useful IC will light up to 10 LEDs (bar mode) or 1 of 10 LEDs (dot mode) in response to an input signal. It can accept an AC or DC signal without extra components for rectification which makes it a very versatile IC. See Fig. I-36.

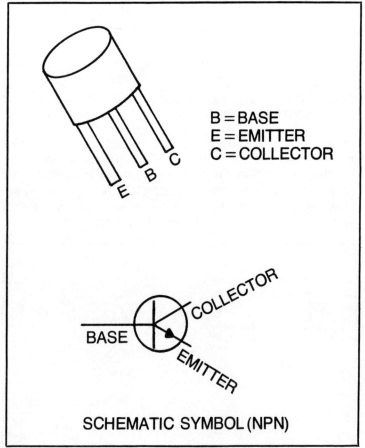

B = BASE
E = EMITTER
C = COLLECTOR

COLLECTOR

BASE

EMITTER

SCHEMATIC SYMBOL (NPN)

Fig. 1-35. An NPN transistor.

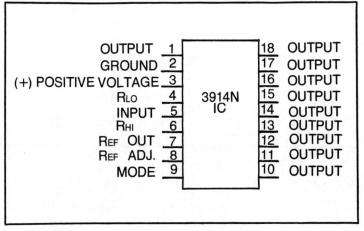

Fig. I-36. The LM3914N bar/dot display driver IC.

4017 DECADE COUNTER IC

This IC is used to turn on LEDs in a sequential pattern. It needs only a clock input pulse (555 timer pulse generator) and a 3-15 volt power supply to work. This is the most important IC in this book.

Incidentally, you can "pulse" the 4017 decade counter manually with a touch switch circuit and control devices by wiring the output pins of the decade counter to resistors or different values all going to a device such as an LED. When you touch the touch wires, the LED will get brighter and brighter with each succeeding touch. See Fig. I-37.

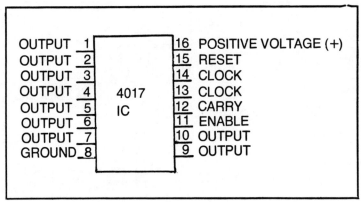

Fig. I-37. The 4017 decade counter IC.

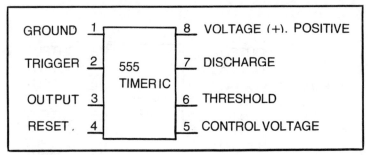

Fig. I-38. The 555 timer IC.

555 TIMER IC

The 555 timer IC is the first and still the most popular IC timer. Many books have been written on this one device. It is used as a clock input pulse generator for the 4017 decade counter IC. See Fig. I-38. The circuit shown in Fig. I-39 can be used to flash LEDs. The potentiometer (R1) controls the pulse rate.

7473 J-K FLIP FLOP IC

The 7473 flip flop IC provides a way to control a circuit's on-off function with just a momentary closing of a switch. By using just one output, you can turn a device on by closing a switch momentarily. To turn it off, close the switch again. This IC works well with the touch switch circuit. See Fig. I-40.

In Fig. I-40 the flip flop IC is wired to "toggle". That is, it will change its output state with every clock pulse. You can simulate a clock pulse by touching its clock lead to ground momentarily.

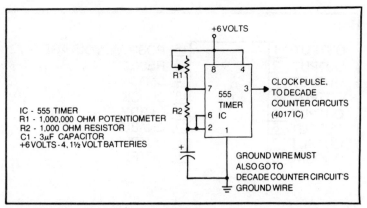

Fig. I-39. A 555 timer IC pulse generator circuit.

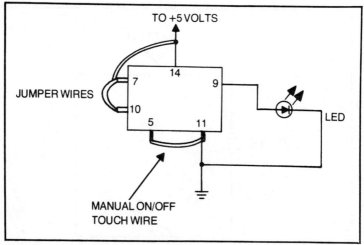

Fig. I-40. On/off circuit diagram.

By the way, there are *two* flip flop ICs in every 7473 IC package. Both of the ICs share the same positive and negative pin connections. See Fig. I-41.

You can connect a touch switch circuit in between the clock pulse pin and the negative (ground) pin and control devices with an on/off touch switch! Very useful and very simple.

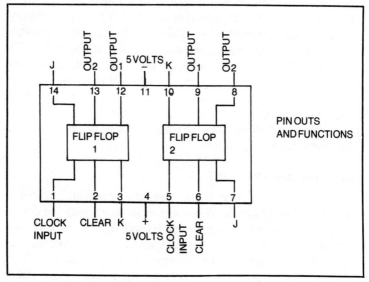

Fig. I-41. 7473 J-K flip-flop.

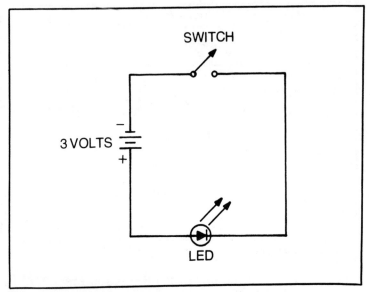

Fig. I-42. Simple switched circuit.

TOUCH CONTROL FOR DISCO DEVICES

Here's a simple way to control some of the projects with a touch of your finger. Wire two NPN transistors as shown. As an example, I have shown two simple circuits. Figure I-42 is a simple series circuit- LED, battery and switch. Figure I-43 is like the first except it substitutes the two transistors in place of the switch. When you touch the *touch control wires* with your finger, the LED will light. The touch wires can be attached to any metal objects and when they are touched the device controlled will turn on.

Since transistors are physically small in size and they don't drain much power from the circuit they are controlling, and make excellent switches for miniature and portable projects, such as bracelets, pendants and belts.

DELAY OFF, ADD-ON CIRCUIT

If you want to delay the turn off of a device after power is removed, simply wire a potentiometer in series with the device and an electrolytic capacitor in parallel with it. See Fig. I-44. You can adjust the delay with the potentiometer's wiper control. It is advisable to use an electrolytic capacitor with a value of at least 2000 μf (microfarad) and a potentiometer with a maximum resistance of at least 1 meg ohm.

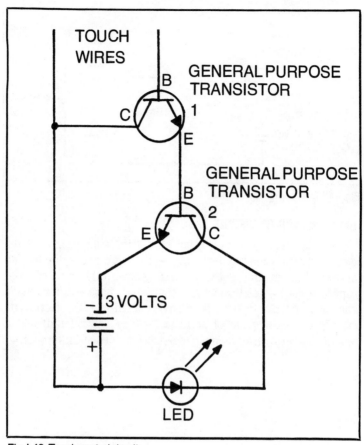

Fig. I-43. Touch control circuit.

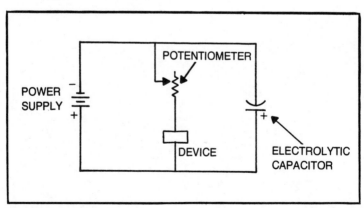

Fig. I-44. Delay off circuit.

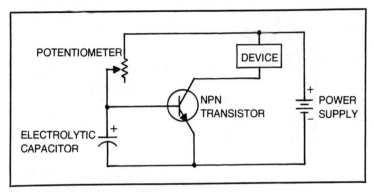

Fig. I-45. Delay on circuit.

DELAY ON, ADD-ON CIRCUIT

When a turn-on delay is required, add this simple circuit to the device. As shown in Fig. I-45, the electrolytic capacitor is charged slowly through the potentiometer. Once fully charged, the capacitor discharges through the transistor's base emitter circuit and turns on the device. It is advisable to use an electrolytic capacitor with a value of at least 2000 uf (microfarad) and a potentiometer with a maximum resistance of at least 1 meg ohm.

Section II

Projects

1

LED VIP Signaler

If you ever want to have a way to know who is trying to gain entrance to your room, office, party, etc., here's a way to tell the guests who are wanted from the unwanted. Place a reed switch in a thin plastic box and position it outside your door in an area where it will not be easily seen. Give the people you may want to visit you a small magnet and they can actuate the reed switch and alert you that they are "preferred" company. Wire the reed switch in series with a battery pack, LED and/or buzzer. See Figs. 1-1 and 1-2.

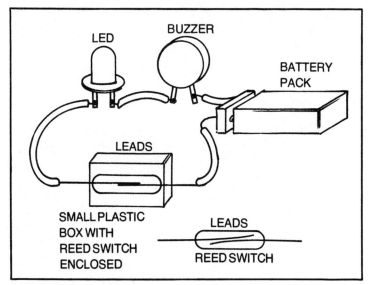

Fig. 1-1. VIP signaler circuit.

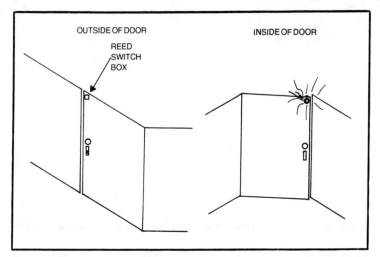

Fig. 1-2. Installing the VIP signaler.

2
Alternately Flashing
Digital Initial Display Box

By using two flasher ICs, you can make each initial flash on and off
independently of each other.

Wire each digital LED to a flasher IC and capacitor and
connect the two circuits to the same mini battery pack. See Figs.

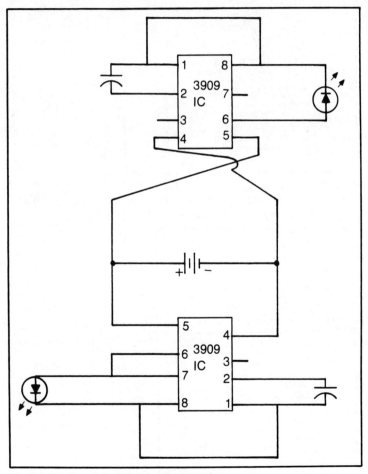

Fig. 2-1. Flashing digital initial circuit schematic.

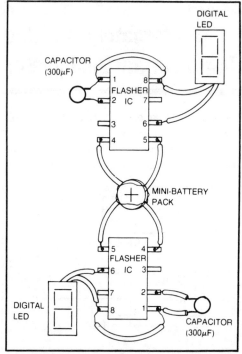

CAPACITOR
(300μF)

1 8
FLASHER
2 IC 7

3   6

4   5

DIGITAL
LED

MINI-BATTERY
PACK

5 4
FLASHER
6 IC 3

7   2

8   1

DIGITAL
LED

CAPACITOR
(300μF)

Fig. 2-2. Flashing initial
wiring diagram.

2-1 and 2-2. Add the type of switch of your choice (reed switch,
mercury switch, etc.) and house the components in a small display
box with a cut-out window as shown in Fig. 2-3.

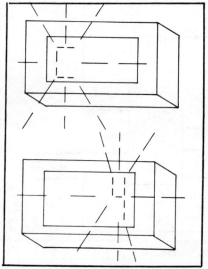

Fig. 2-3. Display box with window.

3
Wall Design

If you happen to be redecorating a room, you might want to install LEDs on a wall before you panel or wallpaper. With the right pattern, this effect will have a fascinating eye appeal for your guests. See Figs. 3-1 through 3-3.

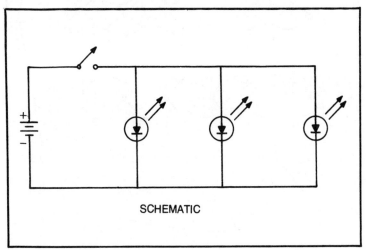

SCHEMATIC

Fig. 3-1. Wall design schematic.

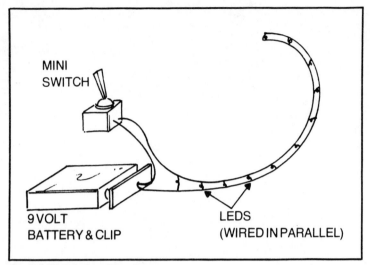

Fig. 3-2. Wall design wiring diagram.

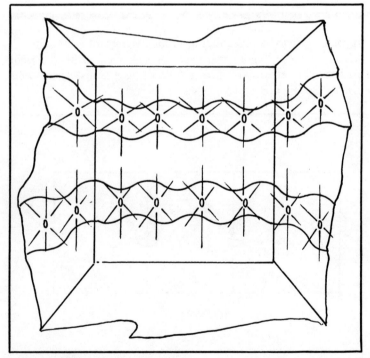

Fig. 3-3. Installing the wall design circuit.

4
Pet Jewelry

Here's a way to show people (and their pets) that even your pet is up to date with his own disco collar.

Attach a flashing, mini battery pack and a mini switch to your pet's collar as shown in Figs. 4-1 and 4-2. This device makes it easy to find your pet (especially a cat) when it's hiding. See Fig. 4-3.

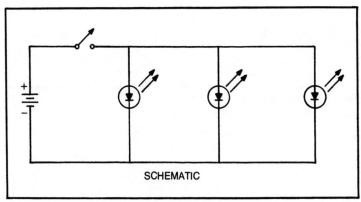

SCHEMATIC

Fig. 4-1. Pet jewelry circuit schematic.

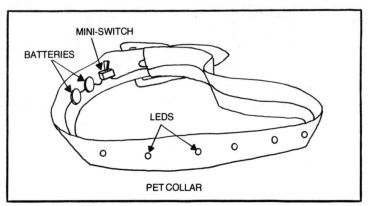

Fig. 4-2. Pet collar.

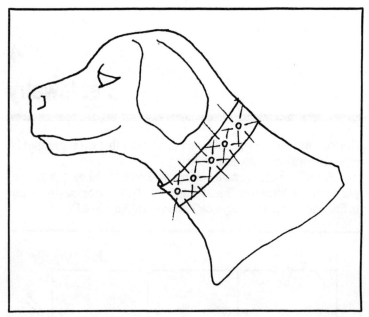

Fig. 4-3. Pet wearing collar.

5
Tie Clip

An illuminating addition to a man's wardrobe can be constructed with an LED, mini battery pack and a mini switch. See Figs. 5-1 and 5-2.

This piece of jewelry should be worn only on appropriate occasions such as at discos and parties. It should accent your attire, not make it appear comical or flashy. See Fig. 5-3.

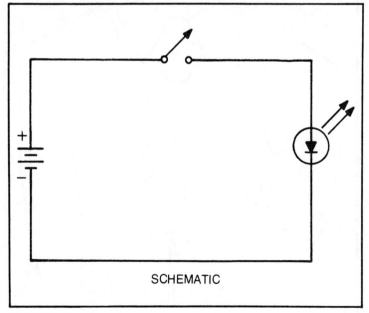

SCHEMATIC

Fig. 5-1. Tie clip schematic.

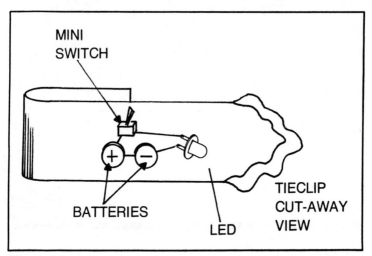

Fig. 5-2. Tie clip circuit diagram.

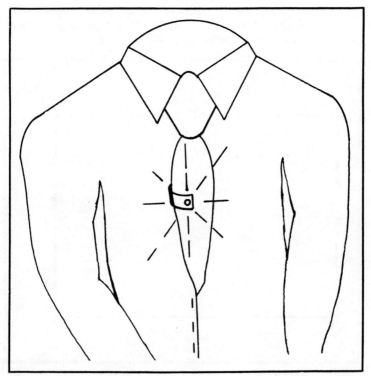

Fig. 5-3. Wearing the tie clip.

6
Buttons

Even the buttons on your shirt, jacket or vest can sport a stylish look with the aid of LEDs. Thread the LEDs through the button holes and sew the buttons securely to the garment. Wire the mini LEDs—your choice of multicolored, flashing or both in parallel to a mini battery pack placed in the pocket of the garment. See Figs. 6-1 through 6-3.

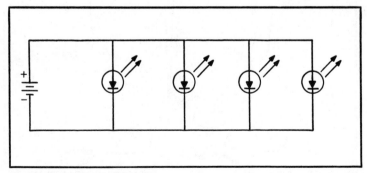

Fig. 6-1. Button circuit schematic.

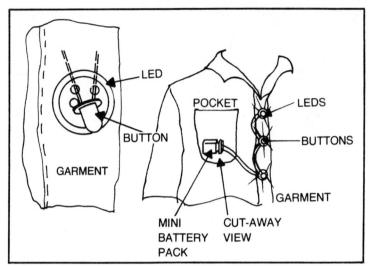

Fig. 6-2. Button wiring diagram.

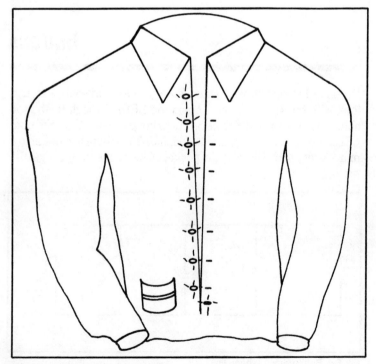

Fig. 6-3. The finished button project.

7
Key Chain Mini-Light

Here's a nice gift that will come in handy. It is not a new invention or concept, but it is very useful and if it is built as small as possible it can be carried all of the time, furthering the chances of its usage.

Simply tape a 1½ volt mini-light with leads to a thin 1½ volt battery. Tape the bared light leads loosely so that they have to be pressed with the finger tips for the light to illuminate. You can insert this device in a wallet, purse or on a keychain for your convenience. See Figs. 7-1 and 7-2.

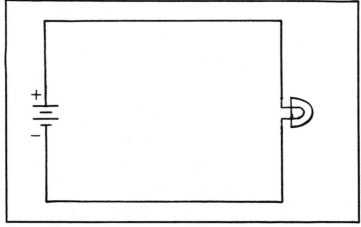

Fig. 7-1. Key chain mini-light circuit schematic.

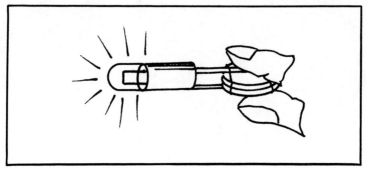
Fig. 7-2. Using the keychain mini-light.

8
Action Bracelet

You can produce a mini disco dance scene on your bracelet with this simple project. Cut out small pictures of dancing figures from a piece of cardboard and cover the cardboard with dark translucent plastic as shown in Fig. 8-1.

Mount the mini decade counter circuit shown in Fig. 8-2 to the top and sides of a bracelet, which has a flat surface area. Place the six LEDs in pairs in position on the face of the bracelet so they will be behind the cut-out figures. See Fig. 8-3. Wire the LEDs so they will display the dancing figures in sequences that will look like action is taking place. Cover the bracelet with decorative material cloth. See Fig. 8-4. Now while you are dancing and partying, your wrist bracelet will mimic your activity. See Fig. 8-5.

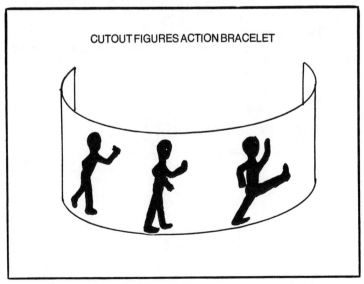

CUTOUT FIGURES ACTION BRACELET

Fig. 8-1. Dancing figures made from cardboard.

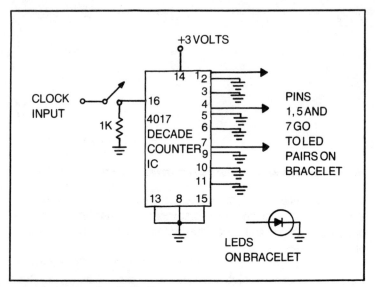

Fig. 8-2. 4017 decade counter IC.

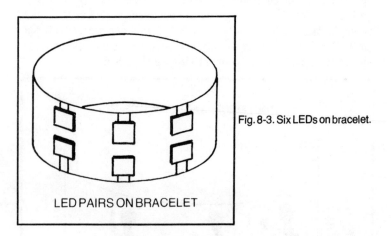

Fig. 8-3. Six LEDs on bracelet.

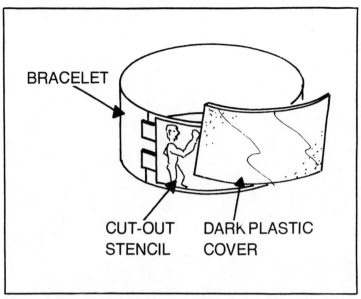

BRACELET

CUT-OUT STENCIL

DARK PLASTIC COVER

Fig. 8-4. Covering the bracelet with plastic or cloth.

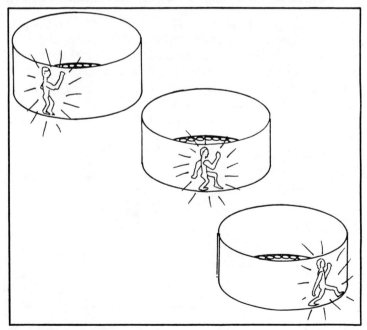

Fig. 8-5. The bracelet in use.

9
LED Toy Gun

Here's a way to add futuristic appeal to a simple toy. Add a pot, battery pack and three flashing LEDs wired in series to the toy weapon. See Fig. 9-1. Mount the LEDs in the barrel and the pot near the gun's trigger. The battery pack can be mounted inside the gun. See Fig. 9-2. This simple modernization will bring new life to an old toy. See Fig. 9-3.

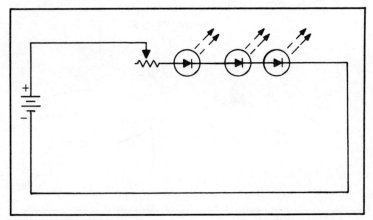

Fig. 9-1. Toy gun circuit schematic.

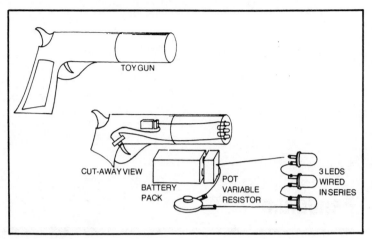

Fig. 9-2. Toy gun wiring diagram.

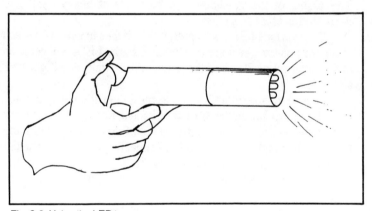

Fig. 9-3. Using the LED toy gun.

10
Pendulum

This pendulum will be a nice addition to your next get together. The casing of the pendulum can be made of heavy cardboard decorated and taped together.

Wire various LEDs with mercury switches in parallel to each other and position the mercury switches so the LEDs will come on in the different positions of the pendulum's swing. See Figs. 10-1 and 10-2.

Feed the battery leads outside the top of the pendulum and twist them around the support wire or chain. Connect a battery pack to the lead wires and position it out of sight. You will turn the lights on the pendulum on and off by connecting the battery pack to its clip so no switch is needed. See Fig. 10-3.

Mount the pendulum on your room ceiling and let it swing! See Fig. 10-4.

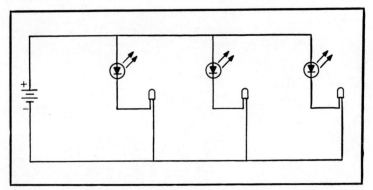

Fig. 10-1. Pendulum circuit schematic.

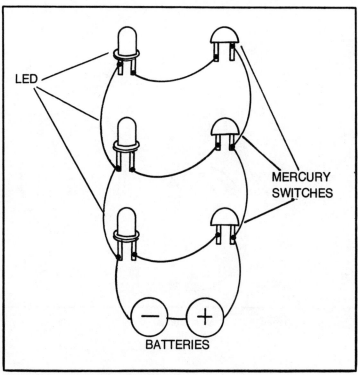

Fig. 10-2. Pendulum wiring diagram.

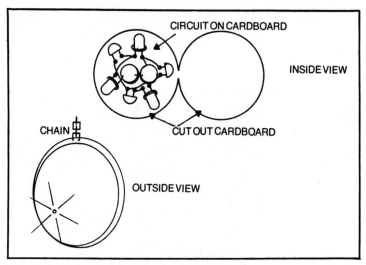

Fig. 10-3. Mounting the circuit on the pendulum weight.

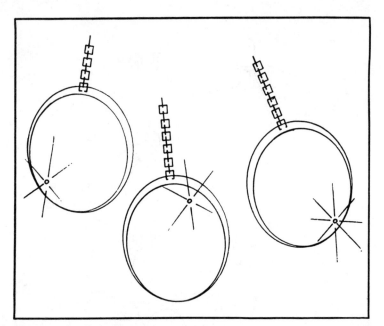

Fig. 10-4. Lights change as pendulum swings.

11

Digital Initial Pet Collar

You can give your pet that distinctive and modern look with his own digital initial jewelry. Wire a digital LED to spell out his initial and wire it in series to a mini battery pack and a mini switch. See Figs. 11-1 and 11-2. Attach the components securely to the pet collar and cover it with material cloth as shown in Fig. 11-3.

Now let your pet show the world his display of electronic pride!

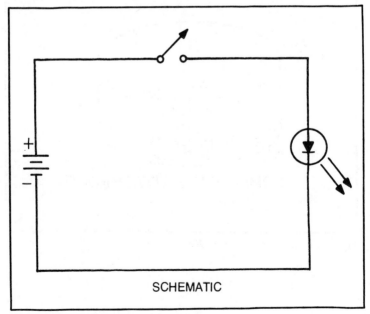

SCHEMATIC

Fig. 11-1. Digital initial pet collar circuit schematic.

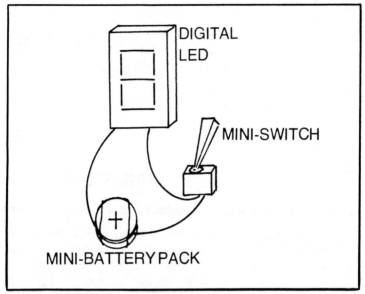

Fig. 11-2. Digital initial pet collar wiring diagram.

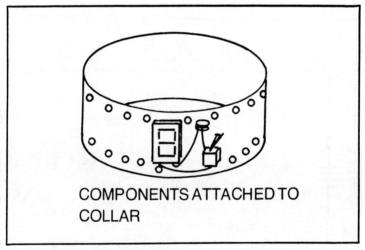

COMPONENTS ATTACHED TO
COLLAR

Fig. 11-3. Attach the circuit to the collar.

12

LED Bead Curtains

If you want the entrance to your room to have a different look hang these curtains up in the doorway and "turn on" your vistors as they enter. Simply buy a set of bead or string curtains and attach LEDs (flashing and multicolored) to the beads with thin insulated wire that is color keyed to the beads. See Figs. 12-1 and 12-2.

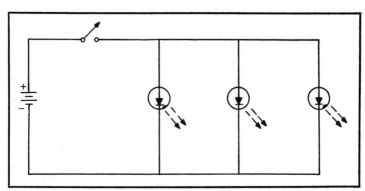

Fig. 12-1. LED bead curtain circuit schematic.

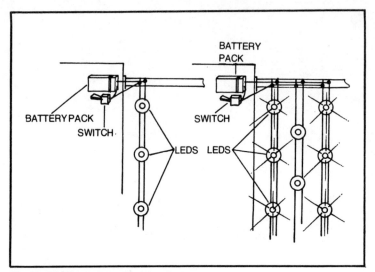

Fig. 12-2. LED bead curtain wiring diagram.

13
LED Toy Car Accent

You can add new life to toys that have become boring and "old" to young ones with this project. By adding either two LEDs to the headlamp area of the car or a single flashing LED to the top, the vehicle will be almost like a new toy to the tot. See Fig. 13-1 and 13-2. If the car has a battery in it (for a motor) you can tap off the existing power supply; if not, use thin watch batteries for the LEDs to keep the weight down. See Fig. 13-3.

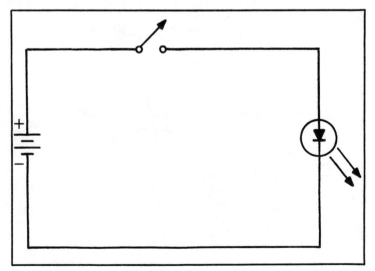

Fig. 13-1. LED toy car accentor schematic.

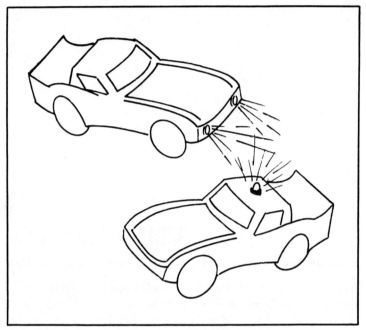

Fig. 13-2. Use LEDs for headlights or a flashing LED on top.

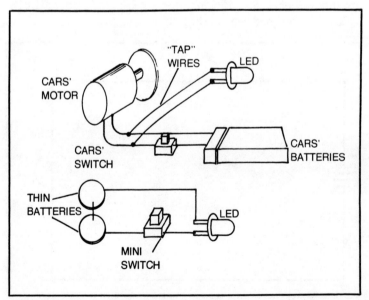

Fig. 13-3. Two different ways to power the LEDs.

14
Blacked Out Poster

This poster design can add a little mystery to your social gatherings. It is a series of LEDs flashing behind an art design cut-out, which is in back of a piece of translucent plastic. See Fig. 14-1.

Wire the three flasher LEDs in series with three pots and in parallel to a battery pack and a mini-switch. See Fig. 14-2. If you prefer, you can also wire electrolytic capacitors in parallel to the flasher LEDs to give them different flash rates. Draw an art design that is eye appealing such as the one shown in Fig. 14-3 and place the flasher LEDs behind the cut-out portions of the poster design. Cover the poster with the translucent plastic and display it on your wall with the flasher LEDs blinking at sequential flash rates. See Fig. 14-4.

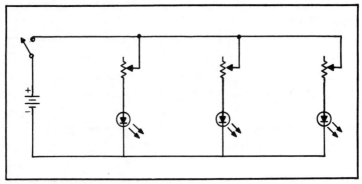

Fig. 14-1. Blacked out poster schematic.

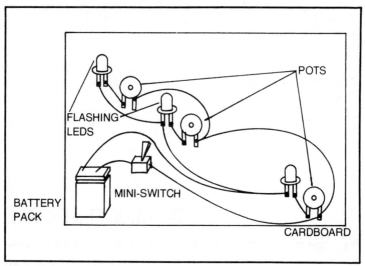

Fig. 14-2. Poster wiring diagram.

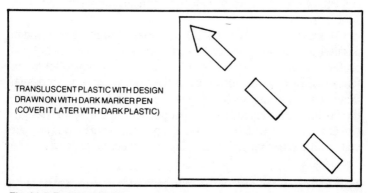

TRANSLUSCENT PLASTIC WITH DESIGN
DRAWN ON WITH DARK MARKER PEN
(COVER IT LATER WITH DARK PLASTIC)

Fig. 14-3. Poster art design.

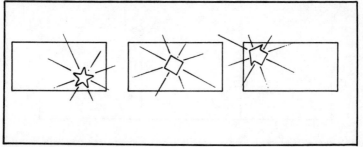

Fig. 14-4. Sequential poster in operation.

15
Handwritten Bracelet

You can produce a more personal display for your bracelet with a handwritten styled name display. This is produced with flat rectangular LEDs underneath a cut-out cardboard stencil of your handwritten name. Wire three rectangular LEDs in parallel to a mini battery pack and a mini switch or a mercury switch. See Figs. 15-1 and 15-2.

Cover the LEDs with your handwritten stencil cut-out and with a sheet of translucent plastic for a "blacked out" appearance when off. Mount the component parts on the face of a bracelet and if you desire, cover them with decorative material cloth. See Fig. 15-3.

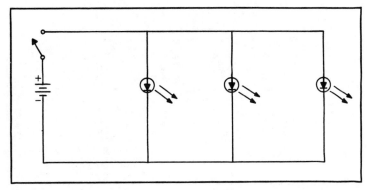

Fig. 15-1. Bracelet schematic.

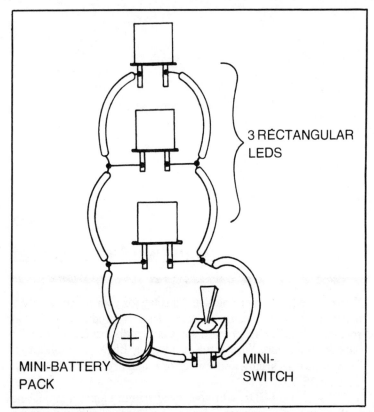

3 RECTANGULAR
LEDS

MINI-BATTERY
PACK

MINI-
SWITCH

Fig. 15-2. Bracelet wiring diagram.

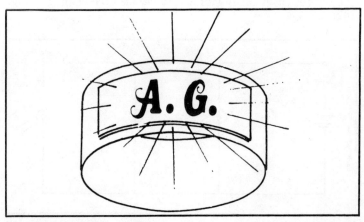

Fig. 15-3. The finished bracelet.

16
Solar Cell Powered LED Reminder

This unique reminder device can be used to remind someone of an important message when it is exposed to light. Wire four 1½ volt solar cells to a flasher LED in series as shown in Fig. 16-1. Write an important message on a piece of heavy cardboard and mount the solar cells at the top of the cardboard or you might prefer to use a separate piece of cardboard for the solar cells. If so, use extra long wire leads for the cells.

Now secure the flasher LED to the back of the message board and punch a small hole for the light to emit through. Place the message board and/or the solar cell board near a room light source and when the lights are turned on, the message will catch the person's attention. See Fig. 16-2.

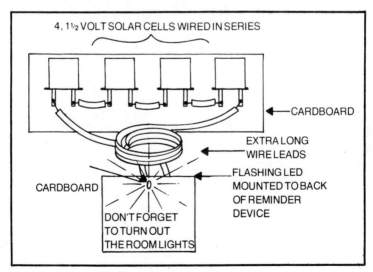

Fig. 16-1. LED reminder circuit diagram.

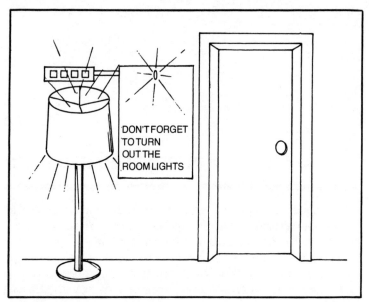

Fig. 16-2. Solar cell reminder installed.

17
Flashing LED Letter Dramatizer

To make a dramatic point at the end of your next important letter, add a flashing LED circuit to it. It is essentially a flashing LED and a mini battery pack constructed flat and neatly placed between two pieces of heavy bond paper. The top sheet will be the one you write your letter on. See Figs. 17-1 through 17-3.

It is advisable to construct this device when you plan to give it to its intended owner to save battery life. No switch is necessary. There's no doubt that it will leave an unforgettable impression on the receiver.

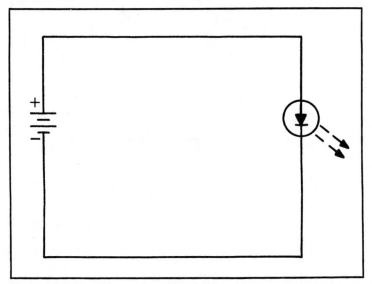

Fig. 17-1. Flashing LED letter dramatizer circuit.

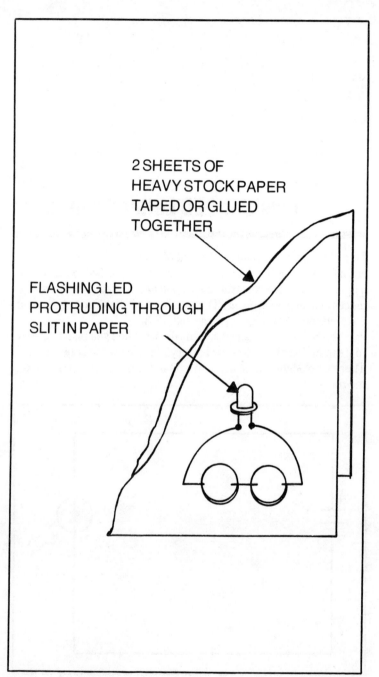

2 SHEETS OF HEAVY STOCK PAPER TAPED OR GLUED TOGETHER

FLASHING LED PROTRUDING THROUGH SLIT IN PAPER

Fig. 17-2. Mounting the LED.

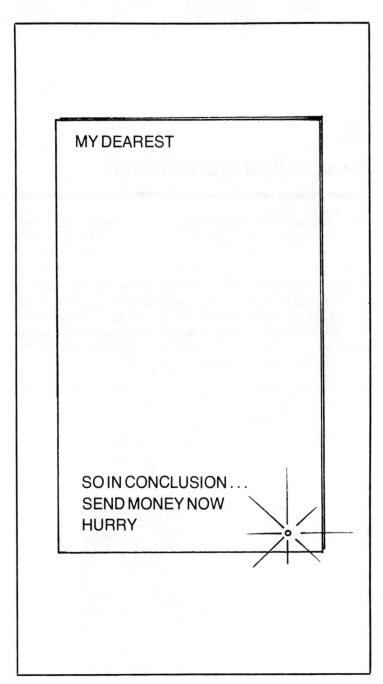

Fig. 17-3. The finished product!

18
Musical Door Ajar Indicator

Imagine your favorite tune being played as you open your car door. Well it's possible and simple thanks to the 4017 decade counter IC. Connect the output pins of the decade counter to pots and to the power lead of a piezo buzzer. Connect the circuit's power lead to the door ajar power wire in the vehicle (located near the door cowl). Ground the circuit's negative leads to the car's ground (any part of the car's frame in the interior). Tune the potentiometer so the piezo buzzer will play a tune in response to the decade counter's pulse rate. See Fig. 18-1. Now the device will play the tune when you open the car door. See Fig. 18-2.

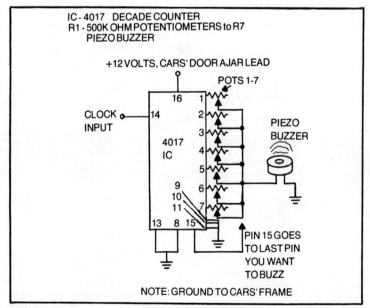

Fig. 18-1. Musical door ajar indicator circuit.

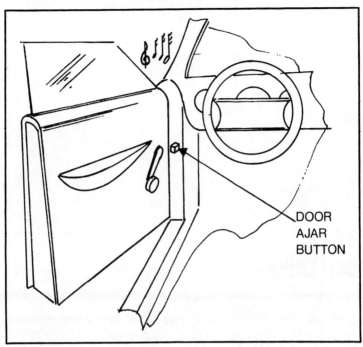

Fig. 18-2. Musical door ajar indicator in operation.

DOOR
AJAR
BUTTON

19
Cuff Links

A unique pair of cuff links can be made with a few miniature components—mini LEDs, a mini switch and a mini battery pack. See Figs. 19-1 and 19-2.

Choose a pair of cuff links with a lot of surface area and mount the mini battery pack on the back of the cuff links. See Fig. 19-3.

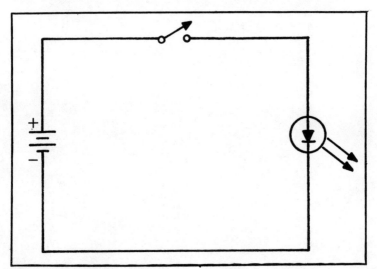

Fig. 19-1. Cuff link schematic.

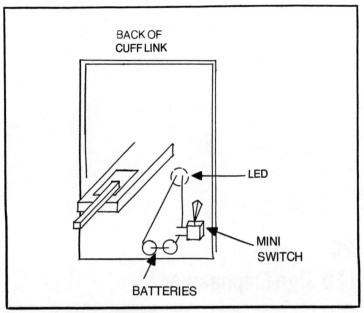

BACK OF
CUFF LINK

LED

MINI
SWITCH

BATTERIES

Fig. 19-2. Cuff link wiring diagram.

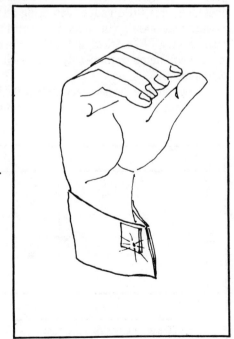

Fig. 19-3. Cuff links in action.

20
LED Sign Emphasizer

Just as the LED chore reminder can alert people to a special message, this little gadget can bring attention to signs already posted that often go unnoticed. Construction is simple and uses two flashing LEDs wired in parallel to a mini battery pack. This device will be on continuously so no switch is needed. See Figs. 20-1 and 20-2.

You can tape the parts securely to the back of the sign with the LEDs placed so their light emits from the sign's sides. See Fig. 20-3.

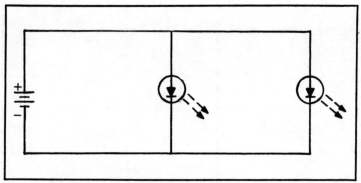

Fig. 20-1. LED sign emphasizer schematic.

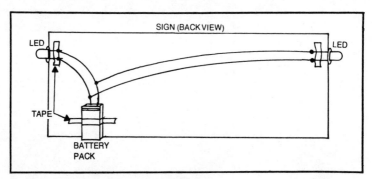

Fig. 20-2. LED sign emphasizer wiring diagram.

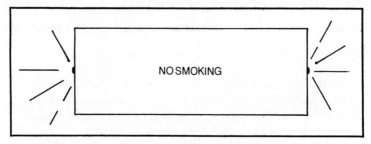

Fig. 20-3. One of the many uses of the LED sign emphasizer.

21
Nighttime LED Auto Spotter

Here's a neat device that will help you locate your car in one of those huge disco parking lots.

Construct, on a heavy piece of cardboard, a flashing LED circuit flasher LED, mini battery pack and mini switch. Place a piece of aluminum foil in back of the LED for maximum brightness. Cut a couple of slits in the cardboard so it can slip onto an auto antenna. See Figs. 21-1 and 21-2.

Now the next time you park your car in a huge lot at night, put the device on your antenna, turn it on and aim it in the direction you are going. See Fig. 21-3.

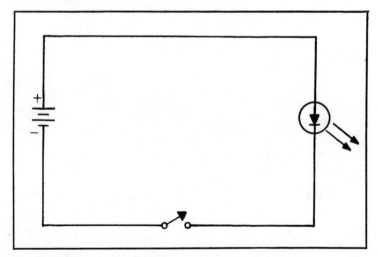

Fig. 21-1. LED auto spotter schematic.

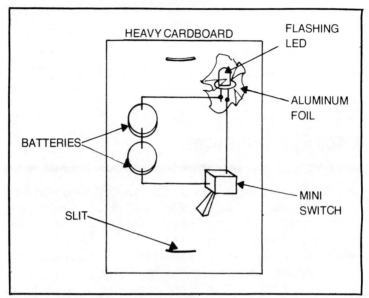

Fig. 21-2. LED auto spotter wiring diagram.

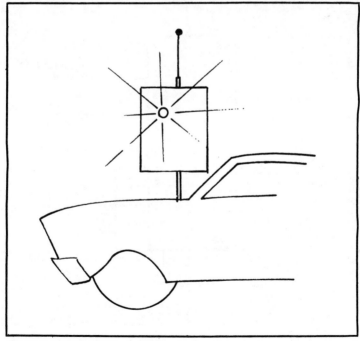

Fig. 21-3. Using the LED auto spotter.

81

22
Door Ajar Indicator

You can have your car produce a mini disco light show when you
enter and exit with this project. Wire a 4017 decade counter to the
positive door ajar switch wire in the car, see Fig. 22-1. Connect the
output pins of the decade counter to four LEDs mounted on the
car's dash, see Fig. 22-2. When you open the door, the LEDs will
flash in sequence in an eye appealing light display.

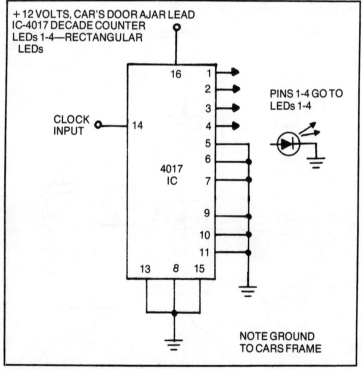

Fig. 22-1. Door ajar indicator schematic.

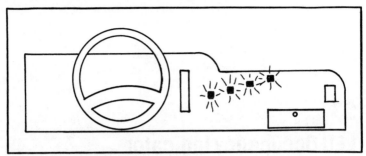
Fig. 22-2. Door ajar indicator in operation.

83

23
LED Occupancy Indicator

In a big household or office, people sometimes venture into rooms already occupied and private. Now this message can be communicated in a discrete manner with a mini-LED placed on the top portion of the door.

Construction is simple and straightforward. Wire a LED in series with a mini-switch and mini-battery pack. See Fig. 23-1. The device should be mounted on the door in such a way that it will blend into its motif when not in operation, see Fig. 23-2.

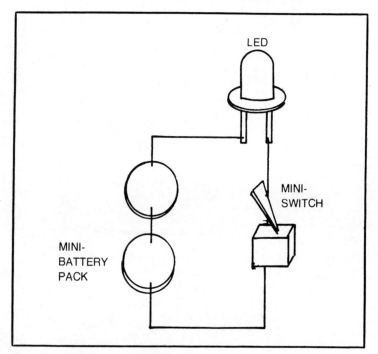

Fig. 23-1. LED occupancy indicator circuit.

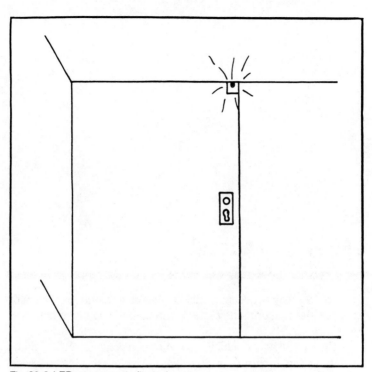

Fig. 23-2. LED occupancy indicator in use.

24
LED Trophy Accent

What better way to accent trophies, awards or emblems than with an LED (flashing or multicolored) guiding the inquisitive onlooker to its location.

Be careful when adding the mini components (LED, mini-switch, and mini-battery pack) to your prize possessions because they can rarely be replaced if damaged. Also, make it easy to replace the battery pack when necessary. See Figs. 24-1 through 24-3.

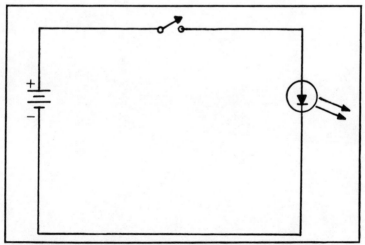

Fig. 24-1. LED trophy accenter circuit schematic.

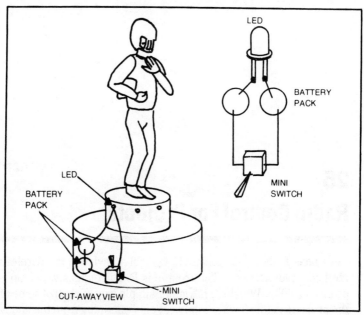

Fig. 24-2. LED trophy wiring diagram.

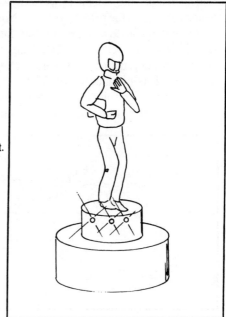

Fig. 24-3. The finished project.

25
Radio Control For Projects

Let's face it, the ultimate way to control a device is the wireless method—radio control. The trouble is R C is expensive, complicated and bulky. Well here is a super simple way to control some of the projects in this book. Simply cut off a mini-plug from the end of an earphone that comes with a portable AM radio. Wire a diode and a transistor to the mini-plug wires as shown in Fig. 25-1. Next wire a small double pole, double throw relay as shown in Fig. 25-2. Affix a piece of wire to the relay's coil lead. Now tune the radio to a point in between stations, plug in the mini-plug and connect the transistor's collector and emitter leads to the device you want to control. When you turn on the relay, it begins to turn on and off like a buzzer. This produces a weak electromagnetic signal that the radio picks up. The diode converts the AC signal energy to DC and turns on the transistor. This turns on your device by radio control.

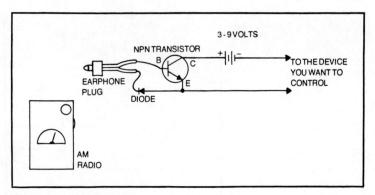

Fig. 25-1. Radio control circuit.

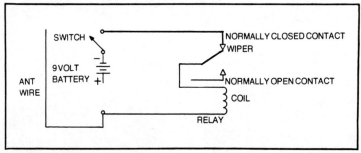

Fig. 25-2. Radio control relay circuit.

26
Flashing LED Wall Switch Spotter

This little gadget will make it easier to find the wall switch in a dark room. It can also be placed to identify objects that might otherwise be stumbled over, or to alert another household member about a certain errand, emergency or message.

Assembly is straightforward using a flashing LED, mini-switch, and mini-battery pack. Decorate the device so it will fit in with the rooms decor and not look too mechanical. See Figs. 26-1 through 26-3.

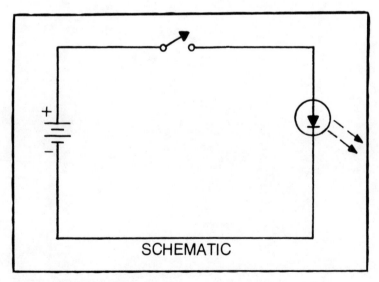

SCHEMATIC

Fig. 26-1. Wall switch spotter circuit.

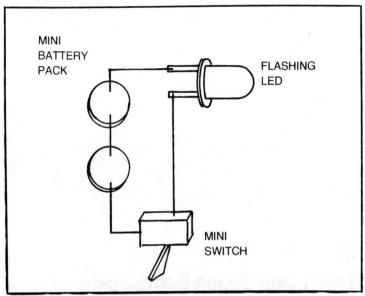

Fig. 26-2. Wall switch spotter wiring diagram.

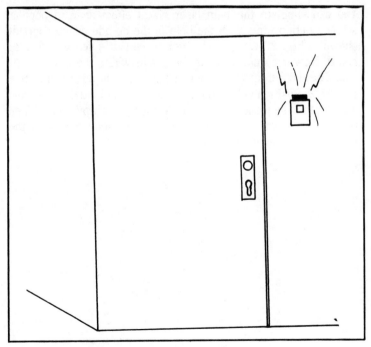

Fig. 26-3. Wall switch spotter in use.

27
Twin Laser Space Battle Poster

You can simulate the twin laser visual effect seen in popular science fiction films with the help of the decade counter circuit shown in Fig. 27-1. Draw an outer space battle scene on poster board. Now cut small holes in the poster where the laser beams would be at different points approaching one of the space ships. See Fig. 27-2. Position yellow rectangular LED s behind the holes and wire them in sequence to the decade counter's output pins. When the switch is on, the LEDs will light in sequence with the appearance of a moving laser beam.

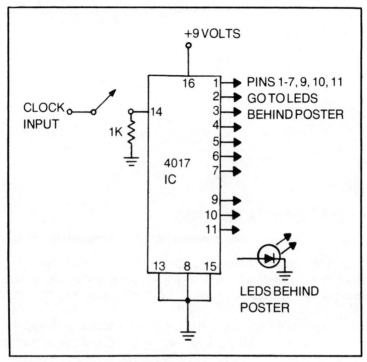

Fig. 27-1. Laser poster wiring diagram.

Fig. 27-2. Poster in action.

28
LED Chore Reminder

If you have a hard time reminding household members (or yourself) about certain chores, then this device will put an end to the flimsy excuses like "it slipped my mind", or "I never saw the note you left".

Simply construct a flashing LED, mini-battery pack and a mini-switch on a small piece of cardboard with a small magnet glued to the reverse side. See Figs. 28-1 and 28-2.

Mount the device on a metallic appliance or cabinet with a note attached and you'll be sure it will get attention. See Fig. 28-3.

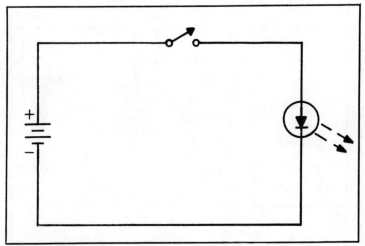

Fig. 28-1. LED chore reminder schematic.

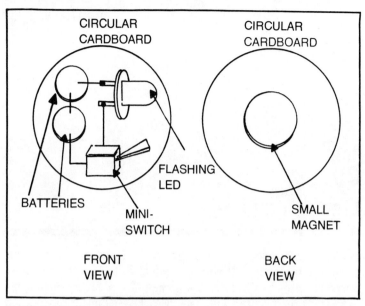

Fig. 28-2. Chore reminder wiring diagram.

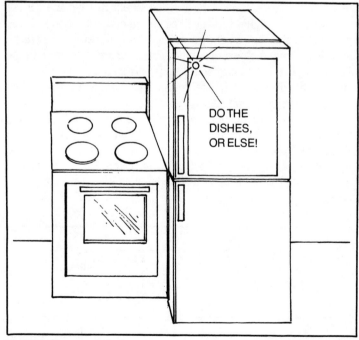

Fig. 28-3. Chore reminder in use.

29
Electronic Dice

A nice modern addition to an old game of chance can be had with these electronic dice. It is basically a circuit of six digital LEDs wired in series to six mercury switches. The six component pairs are wired in parallel to a mini-battery pack. See Fig. 29-1.

Obtain a piece of heavy cardboard and cut it into the shape shown in Fig. 29-2. Tape dark translucent plastic over the cut-out holes where the digital LEDs will be positioned and secured. Now, construct the circuit as shown in Fig. 29-3. Carefully wire each LED to spell out a different number from 1 to 6 and mount it in the plastic window of the cardboard so its display is facing outward. Position the mercury switch with each LED so it will turn on when its side falls in an upright position.

Carefully fold and tape the cardboard so it will form a box shape and test to see if each LED lights when its side is up. When they all test correctly, tape the box together securely. See Fig. 29-4. Now make another electronic die in the same manner and you'll be able to play your games with a modern pair of electronic "bones".

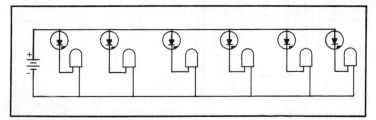

Fig. 29-1. Electronic dice schematic.

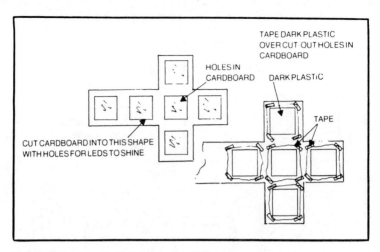

Fig. 29-2. Cardboard pattern for electronic dice.

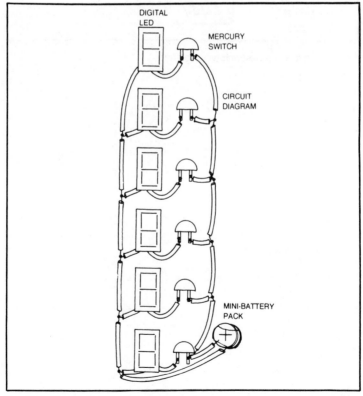

Fig. 29-3. Electronic dice wiring diagram.

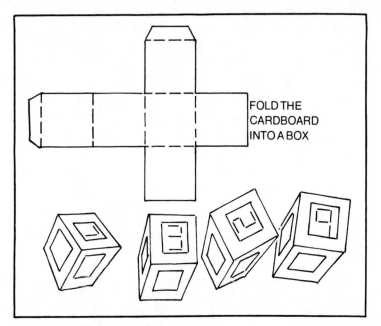

FOLD THE CARDBOARD INTO A BOX

Fig. 29-4. Putting the electronic dice together.

30
Digital LED Shirt Clip

You can make a portable version of the digital initial box to wear on your shirt or jacket. Wire two digital LEDs to spell out your initials and connect them in parallel to a mini-battery pack and a mini-switch. See Figs. 30-1 and 30-2.

Mount the components to a piece of thick plastic and cover the components with a piece of material cloth. Attach a safety clip to the back of the plastic so it can be easily attached to a garment. See Fig. 30-3. Now you'll have a quickly fastened portable initial clip for your clothes.

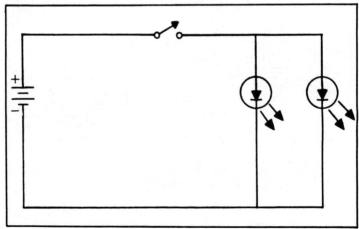

Fig. 30-1. Shirt clip schematic.

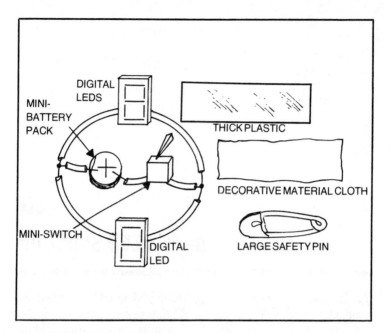

Fig. 30-2. Shirt clip circuit diagram.

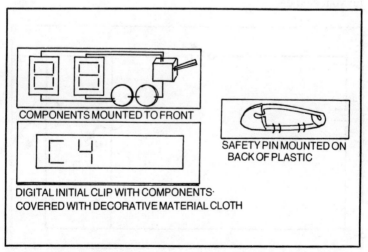

Fig. 30-3. Finishing the LED shirt clip.

Digital Initial Headpiece

You can display your initial digitally on your favorite hat with the help of a digital LED, mini-battery pack and mini-switch combo. Wire the components in series and connect them to a piece of cardboard. Cover the parts with a piece of decorative material cloth. See Figs. 31-1 and 31-2.

Attach small snap fasteners to the hat and the cardboard so the device can be easily removed from the hat when you want to have it cleaned. See Fig. 31-3. Now just snap the cardboard circuit board on the hat and flick the switch!

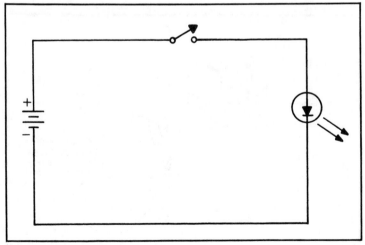

Fig. 31-1. Initial headpiece schematic.

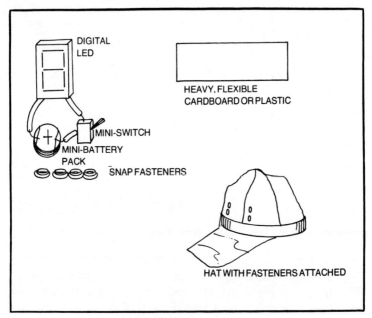

Fig. 31-2. Initial headpiece wiring diagram.

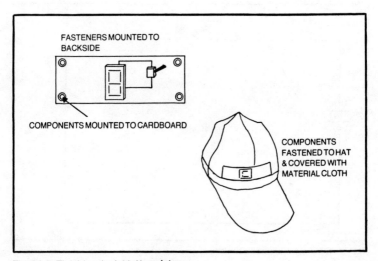

Fig. 31-3. Finishing the initial headpiece.

32
Comb

Since everybody likes to look their best when at a social gathering, this addition to your grooming tools will surely sparkle everyone's attention.

Wire two flasher LEDs and mercury switches in parallel to a mini-battery pack and mini-switch. See Figs. 32-1 and 32-2. Obtain a large comb and attach the components to it with decorative tape leaving small holes for the LED's light to emit through. Position the mercury switches so the LEDs will light up and flash when the comb is in different positions. See Fig. 32-3.

Now when you comb your hair (in public) the comb will produce its own alternating light show and distract everyone's attention from your vanity!

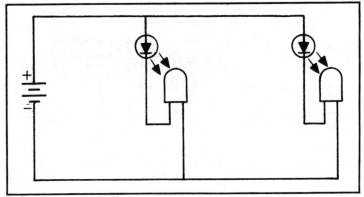

Fig. 32-1. Comb schematic.

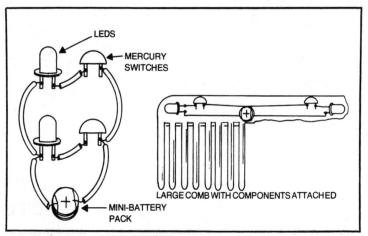

Fig. 32-2. Comb wiring diagram.

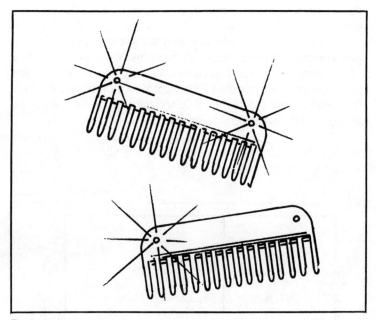

Fig. 32-3. Comb in operation.

LED Refrigerator Reminder

People who wear the latest tight fitting scantily-clad disco outfits probably need all the help they can get trying to keep their weight down. This device will help in that area.

Wire two flasher LEDs in parallel to a mini-battery pack and a normally closed switch as seen in Fig. 33-1 and 33-2. Next, write a short but motivating message on a piece of cardboard and mount the component parts to the back of it. Punch small holes in the cardboard so the LED's light will emit through. Position the normally closed switch on the front of the cardboard reminder so it will contact the inside part of the refrigerator (when the door is closed) and stay in the off position. Now, mount the device on the inside door of the refrigerator so the device comes on automatically when the door is opened. See Fig. 33-3. Now a person will be reminded in a cute and eye catching way to stay fit and trim.

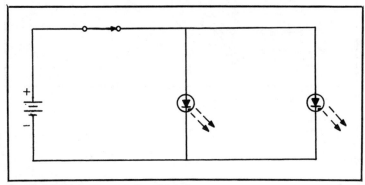

Fig. 33-1. Refrigerator reminder schematic.

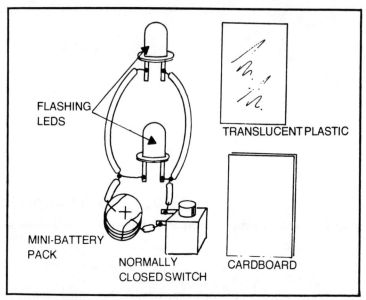

Fig. 33-2. Refrigerator reminder wiring diagram.

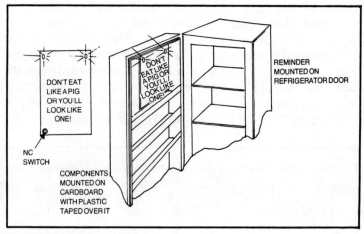

Fig. 33-3. The finished project.

34

Futuristic Electronic Bracelet

This piece of electronic jewelry will make a big hit with science fiction fans since its light display resembles the computer readout display found in many futuristic movies.

Mount three flasher LEDs and three multicolored, rectangular LEDs to the face of a bracelet. Wire each flasher LED to one rectangular LED in series. Now wire the three sets of LEDs in parallel to a mercury switch and three, 1½ volt watch batteries wired in series. See Fig. 34-1. Place a piece of material cloth over the components on the bracelet for a neat look. See Fig. 34-2. Now when you twist your arm in an upright position, the different sets of LEDs will flash in a futuristic light display. See Fig. 34-3.

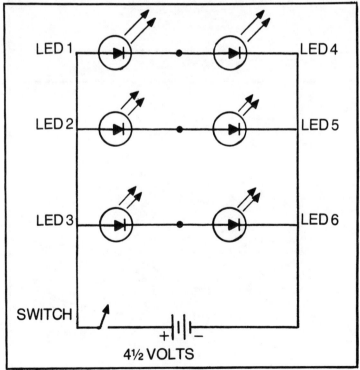

Fig. 34-1. Electronic bracelet schematic.

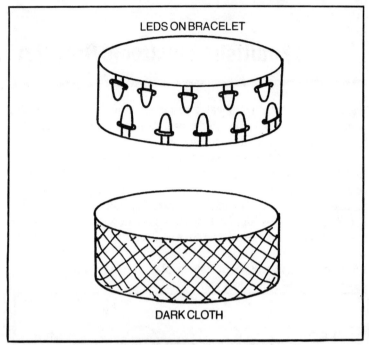

Fig. 34-2. Placing material over bracelet.

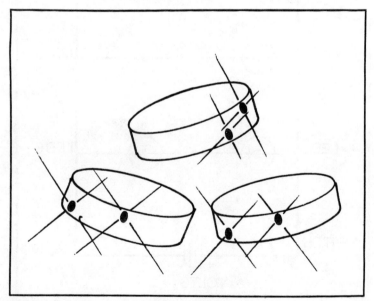

Fig. 34-3. Futuristic electronic bracelet in operation.

35
Futuristic Wall
Design With Light Show

You can simulate the set seen in popular science fiction films with LEDs and construction paper. Cut some various colored shapes out of construction paper in a large and bold futuristic style. You might want to check some science fiction fan magazines for more concepts in these art designs.

Wire two sets of four LEDs (3 multi-colored, 1 flasher) in series and connect the two sets in parallel to a battery pack and mini-switch. See Fig. 35-1. Now cover the LEDs with reflective mirror paper, dark translucent plastic or material cloth. Position this light show circuit in an appropriate position on the futuristic poster. When you turn on the mini-switch, the poster will come to life with a computerized look. See Fig. 35-2.

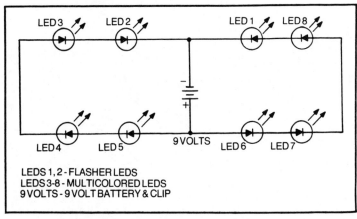

Fig. 35-1. Wall design circuit schematic.

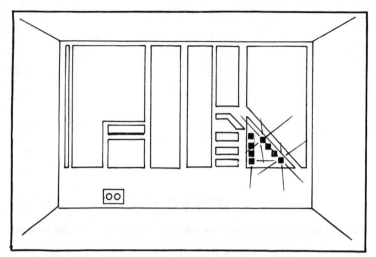

Fig. 35-2. Futuristic wall design with flasher LEDs.

36
Bracelet Reminder Device

We all have some important lesson in life we would like to remember. Sometimes even a picture or a symbol can remind you to do something the right way. You can produce your own personal reminder device with just a few parts.

Wire four flasher LEDs in parallel to a mini-battery pack and a mercury switch as shown in Fig. 36-1. Now cut out the appropriate symbol, picture or word from a piece of cardboard. Place the components and the cardboard stencil on the face of a bracelet. Cover the bracelet with decorative material cloth. Now when you twist your wrist a certain way your important symbol will appear automatically. See Fig. 36-2.

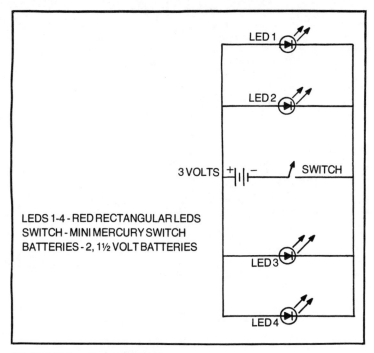

Fig. 36-1. Bracelet reminder circuit.

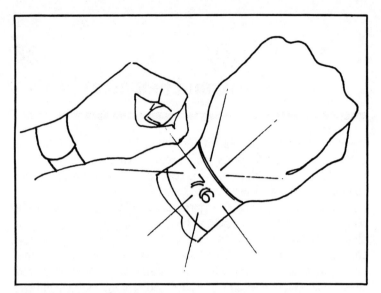

Fig. 36-2. Bracelet reminder in use.

37
Initial Bracelet

This gift will surely bring delight to its new owner. Simply wire two parallel LEDs to a mercury switch and two thin watch batteries as shown in Fig. 37-1. Now cut out the initials of the gift's intended owner from a piece of cardboard so the LED's light can shine through. Cover the cardboard cut-out with dark plastic for a "blacked out" appearance. Mount the parts on the top of a bracelet and cover them (except the dark plastic window) with material cloth. See Fig. 37-2. When the bracelet is tilted upright, the initials will glow through the window. See Fig. 37-3.

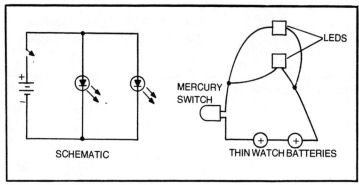

Fig. 37-1. Initial bracelet circuit.

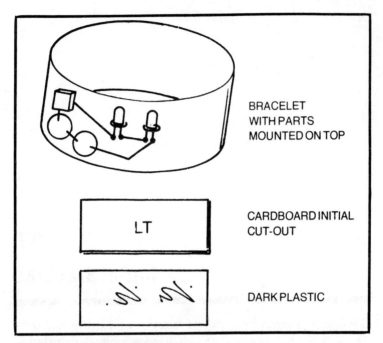

BRACELET
WITH PARTS
MOUNTED ON TOP

CARDBOARD INITIAL
CUT-OUT

DARK PLASTIC

Fig. 37-2. Assembling the initial bracelet.

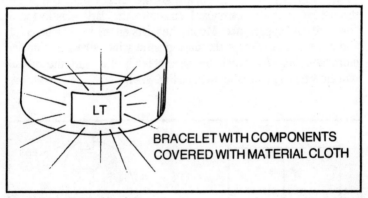

BRACELET WITH COMPONENTS
COVERED WITH MATERIAL CLOTH

Fig. 37-3. The finished product.

38
Digital Message Belt

A novel way to greet friends (or make friends) is to flash a short message to them with a digital message belt. Fasten a couple of digital LEDs, mini-battery pack and mini-switch all wired in series, to the front of a belt buckle. See Figs. 38-1 and 38-2. Of course the digital LED is wired to spell out a short message like HI, BY or ??. Mount the belt buckle on your belt and cover the front of it with decorative material cloth. This project will surely bring lots of envy and admiration for the small amount of construction time spent. See Fig. 38-3.

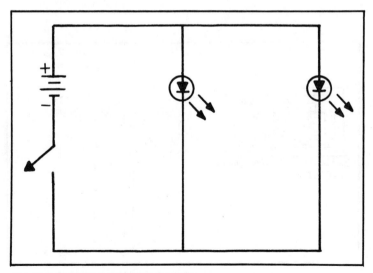

Fig. 38-1. Digital message belt schematic.

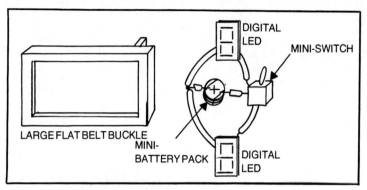

Fig. 38-2. Message belt wiring diagram.

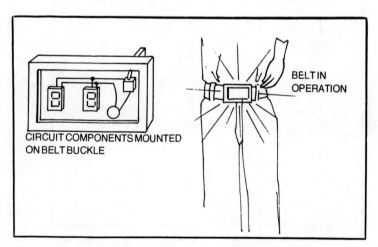

Fig. 38-3. Digital message belt in use.

39

Circular Display Belt

Your waistline can be the life of the party with this easy to build belt. Mount various LEDs on your belt and wire them to the output pins of 4017 decade counter IC. See Fig. 39-1. As the decade counter pulses the LEDs, they will seem to circle your body in an eye appealing manner. You can adjust the speed of this electronic hoola hoop with the pot (R1). See Fig. 39-2.

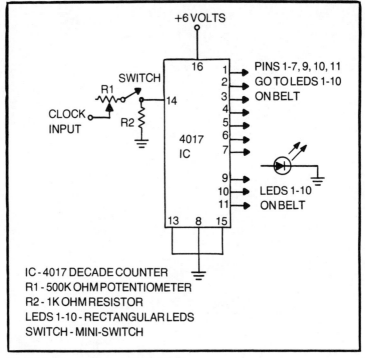

Fig. 39-1. Circular display belt schematic.

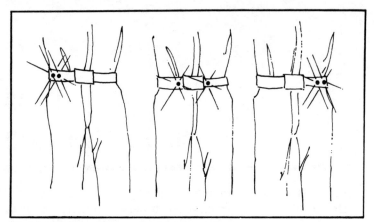

Fig. 39-2. Circular display belt in action.

40
Digital Initial Pendant

You can make an unique pendant that will display digital initials with just a few simple parts. Find a pendant with a large surface area and mount a small digital LED on it that is wired to spell out a person's initial. Wire a mini battery pack and mini switch in series to the LED as shown in Figs. 40-1 and 40-2. Cover the components with decorative material cloth or dark plastic for a blacked out appearance when not in use. See Fig. 40-3.

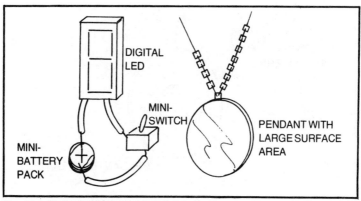

Fig. 40-1. Digital initial pendant circuit.

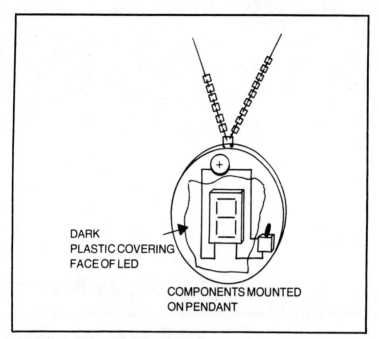

DARK
PLASTIC COVERING
FACE OF LED

COMPONENTS MOUNTED
ON PENDANT

Fig. 40-2. Mounting the circuit on the pendant.

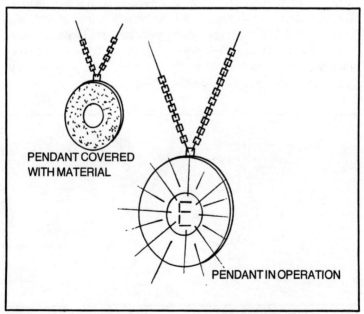

PENDANT COVERED
WITH MATERIAL

PENDANT IN OPERATION

Fig. 40-3. The finished pendant.

41
Pants

Here's a project that produces a very unusual and artistic look when in operation. It is an addition to a pair of pants that will make your every step an illuminating light show.

Wire six LEDs and six mercury switches in parallel to a mini-battery pack as shown in Figs. 41-1 and 41-2. Sew the components inside a piece of long material cloth and attach snap fasteners to the cloth.

Next, attach snap fasteners to the pair of pants you will use and attach the cloth component circuit to the pants. See Fig. 41-3. Now as you walk the LEDs will go on and off in an eye appealing pattern. See Fig. 41-4.

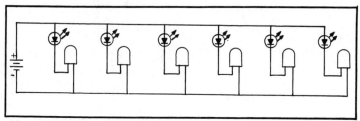

Fig. 41-1. Pants schematic.

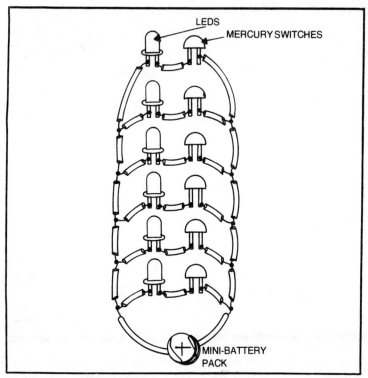

Fig. 41-2. Pants wiring diagram.

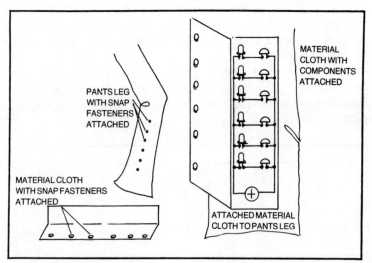

Fig. 41-3. Completing the pants.

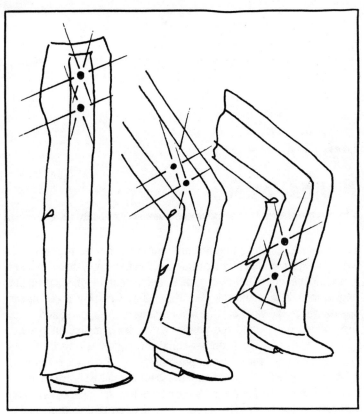

Fig. 41-4. Pants in operation.

42
Motion Poster

You can make posters that are mini movies, that is, they have an eye appealing motion picture effect. As an example, draw an outer space scene complete with stars and a couple of space ships engaging in a laser battle. See Fig. 42-1. Cut tiny holes in the poster where the stars and the laser beams path appears, and cover the holes from behind the poster with dark translucent plastic. Mount various LEDs directly behind the poster where the holes appear and wire them to the output pins of a 4017 decade counter IC as shown in Fig. 42-2. Make sure the laser beam LEDs are wired so they will appear to shoot across the poster in sequence. Now, when you turn on the switch, the poster will have twinkling stars and an action space battle taking place.

Of course you can think of your own moving poster scenes like dancing figures, racing cars, etc.

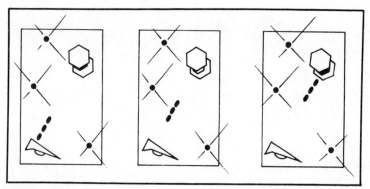

Fig. 42-1. Motion poster.

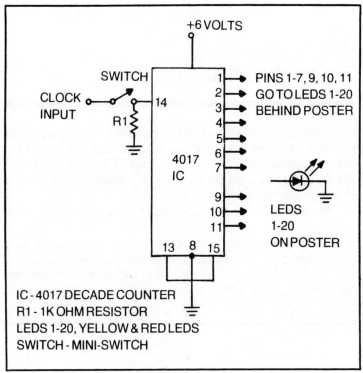

+6 VOLTS

SWITCH

CLOCK
INPUT

R1

14

1 — PINS 1-7, 9, 10, 11
2 — GO TO LEDS 1-20
3 — BEHIND POSTER
4
5
6
7

4017
IC

9
10
11

LEDS
1-20
ON POSTER

13 8 15

IC - 4017 DECADE COUNTER
R1 - 1K OHM RESISTOR
LEDS 1-20, YELLOW & RED LEDS
SWITCH - MINI-SWITCH

Fig. 42-2. Motion poster wiring diagram.

43
Digital Wallet Reminder

An economically valuable gift can be made with a few components that will surely be worth the construction time. Construct the decade counter circuit as shown in Fig. 43-1. Wire the digital display LED to spell out the word "SAVE". Mount the components close together and as flat as possible.

Insert this mini-circuit in the corner of a wallet and cut away a small portion for the LED's light to emit through. Cover this hole with material cloth the same color as the wallet for a neat appearance. Now, whenever you're tempted to spend more than you should, this electronic reminder will help you fight the temptation. See Fig. 43-2.

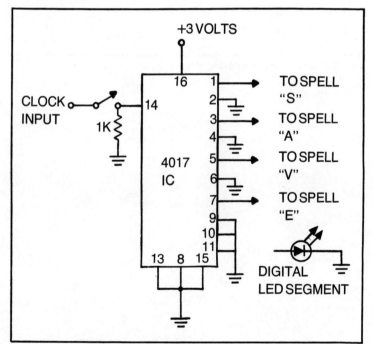

Fig. 43-1. Digital display wallet reminder circuit.

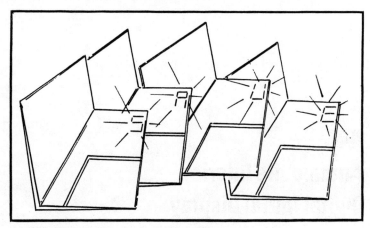

Fig. 43-2. Digital display wallet reminder in use.

44
Automobile Interior
Digital Initial Display

Digital initial displays can add that elegant and modern look to automobile interiors. The best place to mount the digital initial display (in my personal opinion) is on the far right hand side of the dash. There, they are not front and center (and too flashy), yet they are visible and distinctive.

Wire the digital LED segments to display your initials and position them on the dash of your car. Wire a battery pack and mini-switch in series to the LEDs and position them out of sight. See Figs. 44-1 and 44-2.

You should cover the digital LEDs with material cloth that matches your dash's color scheme for a professional appearance. See Fig. 44-3.

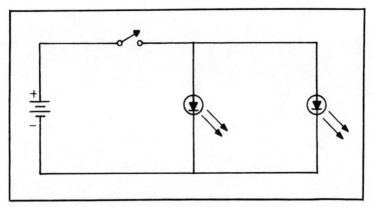

Fig. 44-1. Automobile initial display schematic.

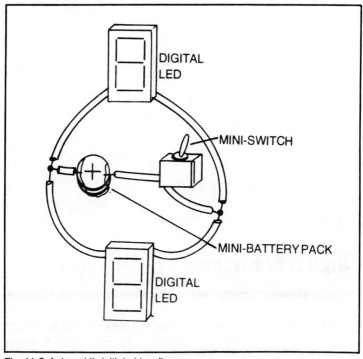

Fig. 44-2. Automobile initial wiring diagram.

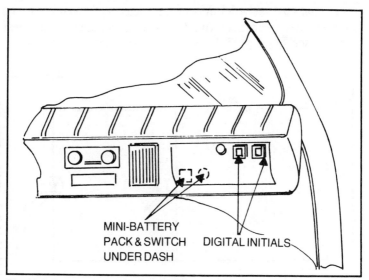

Fig. 44-3. Automobile interior digital initials installed.

129

45
Digital Bracelet

Digital display LEDs can find a home on a person's arm as a unique form of jewelry. Obtain a bracelet that has a large flat surface area. Next, wire two digital LEDs in parallel (spelling out a person's initials) and connect them to a mini battery pack and mini-switch. See Figs. 45-1 and 45-2. Mount the components securely to the bracelet and cover them with decorative material cloth for a neat appearance. See Fig. 45-3.

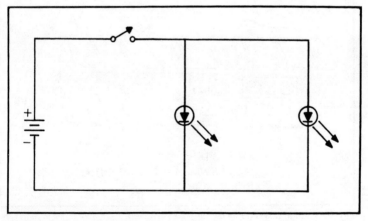

Fig. 45-1. Digital bracelet schematic.

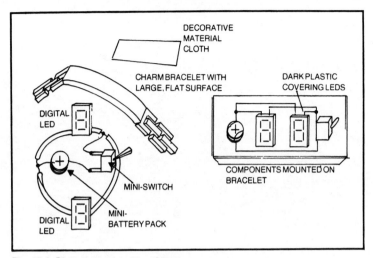

Fig. 45-2. Digital bracelet wiring diagram.

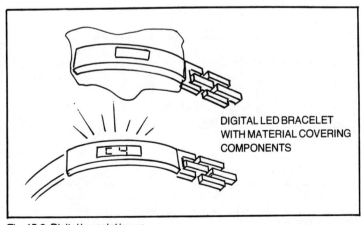

Fig. 45-3. Digital bracelet in use.

46
Barrette

Many women wear small stylish hair combs called barrettes to hold a certain hairstyle in place. If you know a female who likes novel and unique gifts, give her this barrette.

Use very tiny mini LEDs for this project so their light looks like small flickering orbs. Wire the LEDs in parallel with three mercury switches and a mini-battery pack. See Figs. 46-1 and 46-2. In this manner, the lights will turn on in relation to the wearer's head movements. See Fig. 46-3.

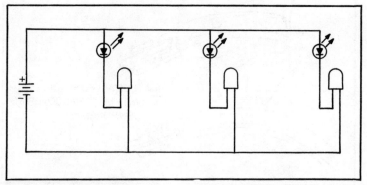

Fig. 46-1. Barrette schematic.

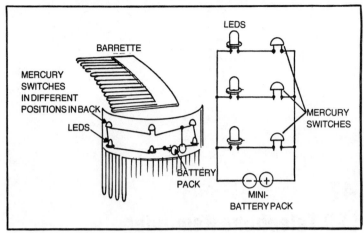

Fig. 46-2. Barrette wiring diagram.

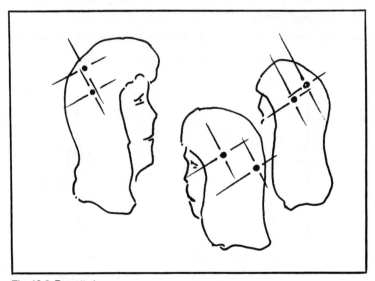

Fig. 46-3. Barrette in use.

133

47
LED Telephone Reminder

In some households and offices, telephone bills can reach outrageous heights. Here's a neat device that will remind all telephone users to keep their calls short and sweet.

Wire a flasher LED in series to a mini-battery pack and a normally closed push-button switch. See Figs. 47-1 and 47-2.

Construct and position the device so it can be placed neatly in the cradle area where the receiver rests. Position the circuit so that the receiver is not off the hook. The receiver should now keep the push-button switch in the off position. See Fig. 47-3.

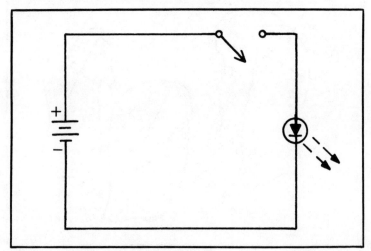

Fig. 47-1. LED telephone reminder schematic.

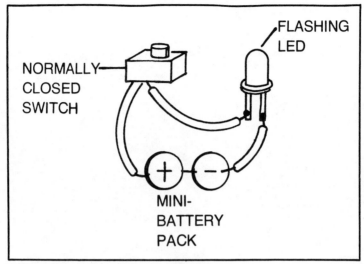

Fig. 47-2. Telephone reminder wiring diagram.

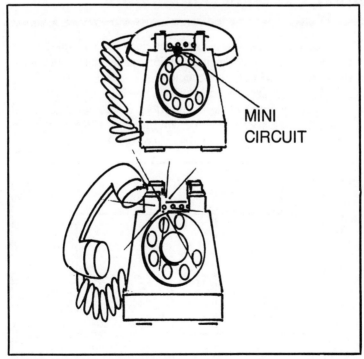

Fig. 47-3. LED telephone reminder in use.

48
Glove Box Light (Automatic)

This gadget is almost invaluable if you don't have a lighted glove box in your car. It will make finding things easier and will double as a small reading light. Wire a couple of mini-lamps in parallel to a mini-battery pack and a mercury switch. See Figs. 48-1 and 48-2.

Secure the components to the door of your glove box and position the mercury switch so it will turn on the lights automatically when the door is in the open position, as in Fig. 48-3.

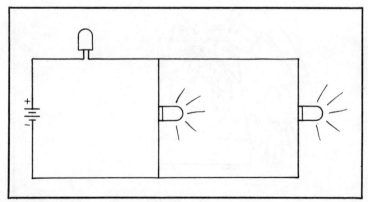

Fig. 48-1. Auto glove box light schematic.

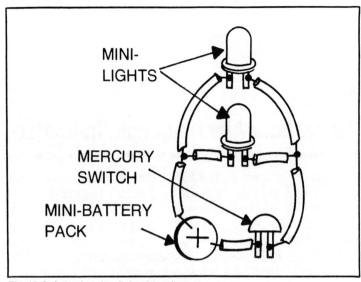

MINI-
LIGHTS

MERCURY
SWITCH

MINI-BATTERY
PACK

Fig. 48-2. Auto glove box light wiring diagram.

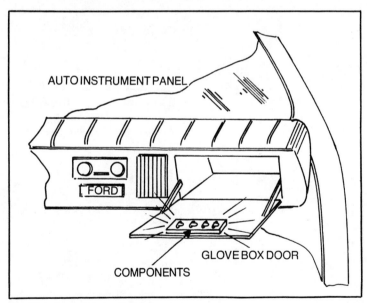

AUTO INSTRUMENT PANEL

FORD

GLOVE BOX DOOR

COMPONENTS

Fig. 48-3. Auto glove box light in use.

49

Digital Door Ajar Reminder/Indicator

You can use a compact digital LED to inform you in a novel way that your car door is open. Wire the 4017 decade counter circuit as shown in Fig. 49-1 and connect the positive lead to the door ajar switch's positive wire. Ground the circuit's negative wire to the auto's ground (and ground wire in the car interior). Now, wire the digital display LED to the decade counter's output pins to spell out the letters D, O, O, R, A, J, A, R in sequence. Place the LED on the car's dash and cover it with material cloth for a neat appearance. See Fig. 49-2.

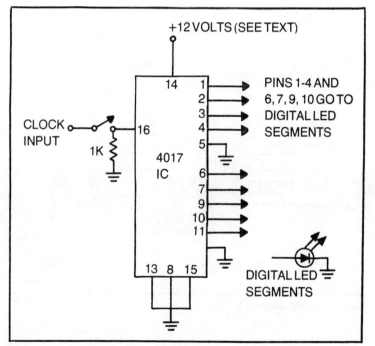

Fig. 49-1. Digital door ajar reminder schematic.

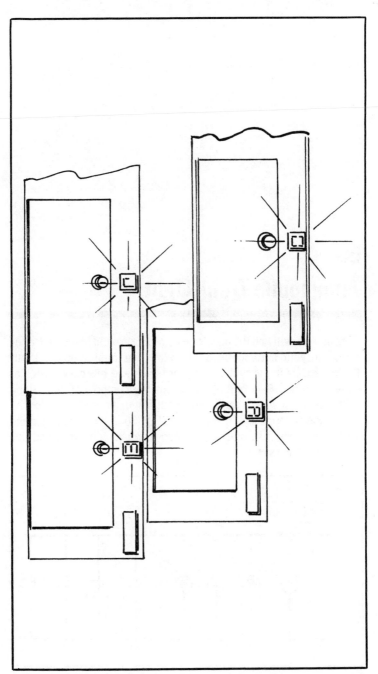

Fig. 49-2. Digital door ajar reminder in use.

50
Automobile Trunk Light

This project will end the problem of groping around in the dark after things in your automobile trunk. Wire four mini-lamps and four flasher LEDs in parallel to a battery pack and mercury switch as shown in Figs. 50-1 and 50-2. Mount the components on a long rectangular strip of cardboard and fasten it securely to the underside of your auto's trunklid. See Fig. 50-3. Now the lamps and LEDs will turn on automatically when you open your trunk and also produce a mini light show as well.

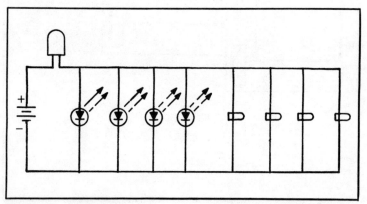

Fig. 50-1. Trunk lights schematic.

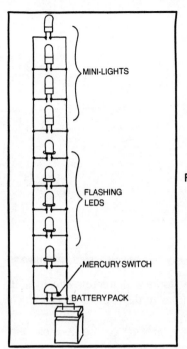

MINI-LIGHTS

FLASHING
LEDS

MERCURY SWITCH

BATTERY PACK

Fig. 50-2. Auto trunk light wiring diagram.

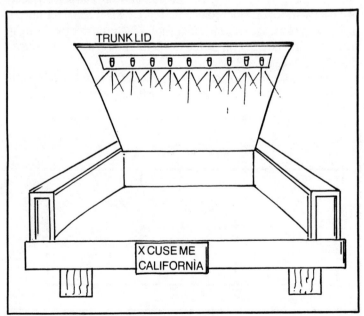

TRUNK LID

X CUSE ME
CALIFORNIA

Fig. 50-3. Trunk lights in use.

51
LED Floor Accent

Many discos and dance halls have floors with lighting effects built into them. You can accent your floor in the same style but much more economically.

Obtain a poster that will look "proper" on the floor of your room's floor (preferably a den or recreation room) and place a piece of clear plastic over it for protection. Place LEDs behind the poster in various positions and punch small holes in the poster for the light to emit. Wire the LEDs in series to a mini-battery pack and switch. See Figs. 51-1 and 51-2.

Now, place the poster on your room floor and secure with carpet tape and turn on your own built-in floor show! See Fig. 51-3.

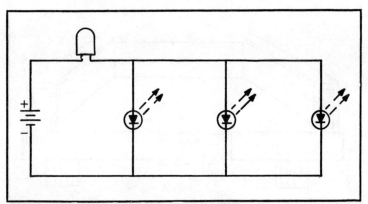

Fig. 51-1. LED floor accenter schematic.

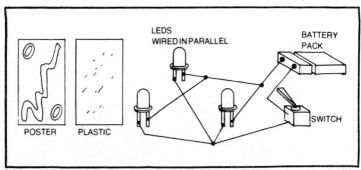

Fig. 51-2. Floor accenter wiring diagram.

Fig. 51-3. Floor accenter in use.

52
Car Maintenance Reminder

This device will help you keep your car in good shape so it won't fail you at critical times. Write a list of preventive maintenance chores you should do to your car every now and then. Cover this list with transparent plastic to protect it from underhood dirt and place two flasher LEDs on either sides of the list. See Figs. 52-1 and 52-2. Wire a mini-battery pack to the LEDs with a mercury switch in series and secure them to the back of the list.

Secure the list on the underside of your car hood where it will be seen. Position the mercury switch so the flasher LEDs will turn on when the hood is raised and the list will remind you to take care of your car in a colorful way. See Fig. 52-3.

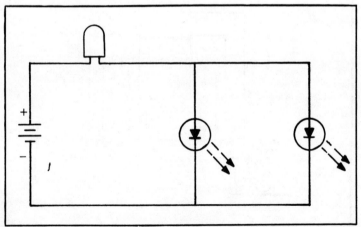

Fig. 52-1. Car maintenance reminder schematic.

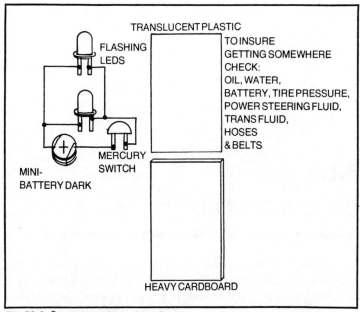

Fig. 52-2. Car maintenance wiring diagram.

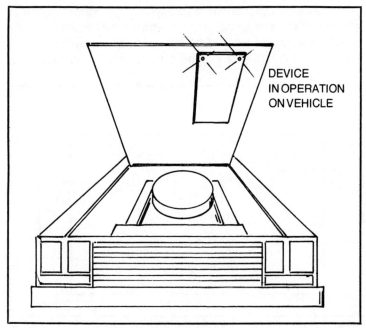

Fig. 52-3. Maintenance reminder in use.

53
Digital Initial Ring

You can add a small but unique addition to your wardrobe with this easy to build project. It is a digital initial ring. Wire a digital LED to spell out your initial and connect it in series to a mini-battery pack as shown in Figs. 53-1 and 53-2. Cut one of the wires in two and bare the ends. This will be your mini-switch.

Mount the components on the top of a ring which has a large and flat surface area. Cover the parts with decorative material cloth and feed the mini wire leads (the switch wires) through the cloth so you can twist them together to turn the ring on. See Fig. 53-3.

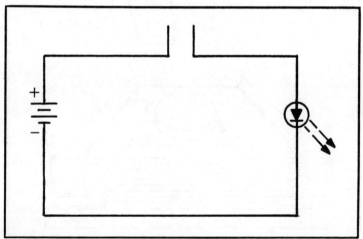

Fig. 53-1. Digital initial ring schematic.

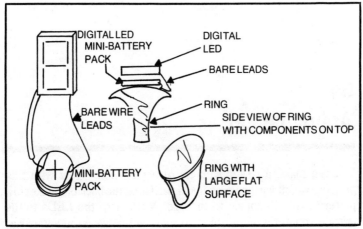

Fig. 53-2. Initial ring wiring diagram.

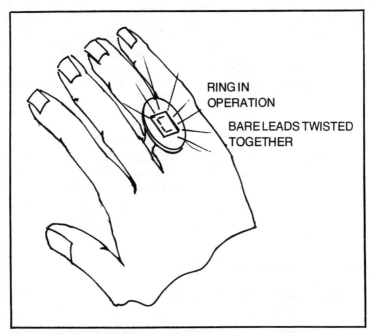

Fig. 53-3. Digital initial ring in use.

54
Action Jacket

You can make a jacket with its own mini light show with this project. Mount various rectangular LEDs on the back of a jacket in a pattern that will appeal to the eye. Next, wire the LEDs to the decade counter's output pins so they will come on in sequence. Place the components in the jacket's pocket and cover the LEDs with material cloth that matches the jacket. Now when you turn on the mini-switch, you'll be your own mobile disco show! See Figs. 54-1 and 54-2.

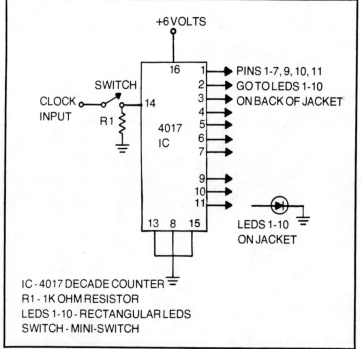

Fig. 54-1. Action jacket wiring diagram.

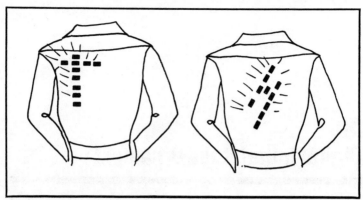
Fig. 54-2. Action jacket designs.

55
Digital Initial Hood Ornament

You can add the look of distinction to your car with this novel project. Wire a digital LED (spelling out your initial), battery pack and mini-switch in series. Use extra long lead wire for the LED as the battery pack and mini-switch will be placed inside of your auto's interior. See Fig. 55-1. Mount the digital LED on a hood ornament and cover it with protective plastic. See Fig. 55-2.

Mount the hood ornament to your auto's hood and lead the wires into your car interior. Mount the battery pack under the dash and the mini switch on the lower part of the dash. Now you can control the electronic hood ornament from the comfort of the driver's seat. See Fig. 55-3.

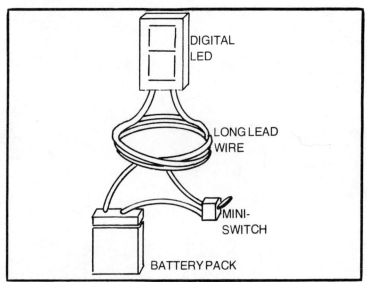

Fig. 55-1. Digital hood ornament.

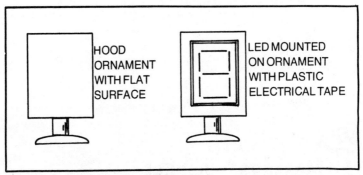

Fig. 55-2. Close-up view of hood ornament.

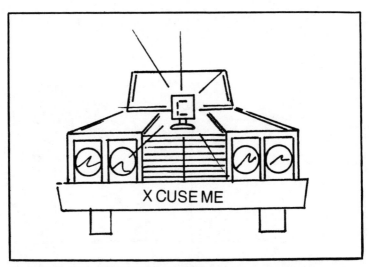

Fig. 55-3. Digital hood ornament in operation.

56
LED Message Reminder

You can be sure to be reminded of important reading assignments with this gadget. Wire two flasher LEDs in parallel to a mini battery pack and mercury switch. Write an important and motivating message on a piece of cardboard and punch two small holes in it for the LED's light to emit through. See Figs. 56-1 and 56-2. Now position the mercury switch so the reminder device will turn on when it is lying flat (like it will be in a book that is lying flat on a table top). Now just slip the LED reminder device into your book and it will flash a silent but eye catching message that it wants to be read. To turn the device off, just turn it over. See Fig. 56-3.

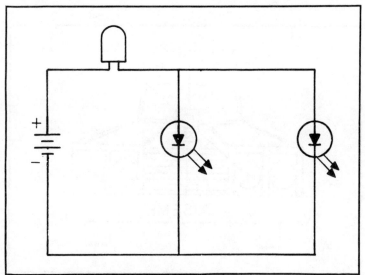

Fig. 56-1. LED message reminder schematic.

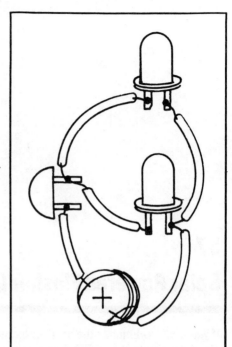

Fig. 56-2. Message reminder wiring diagram.

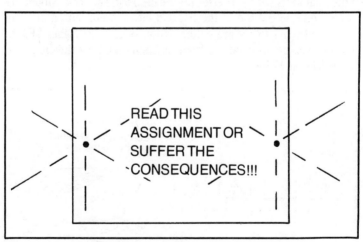

READ THIS
ASSIGNMENT OR
SUFFER THE
CONSEQUENCES!!!

Fig. 56-3. The finished message reminder.

57
Solar Powered Flasher LED Hat

If you want to eliminate the need for battery replacement and add a bit of novelty to your LED disco hat, simply substitute four, 1½ volt solar cells wired in series for the mini battery pack. Mount the solar cells on the top of the hat and cover them with a piece of transparent plastic for protection. Now, secure the flasher LED to the desired position on the front of the hat and it's finished! See Figs. 57-1 and 57-2.

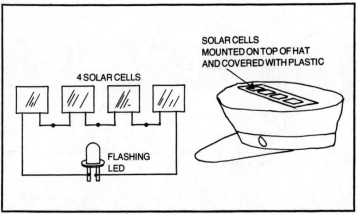

Fig. 57-1. Solar powered LED hat wiring diagram.

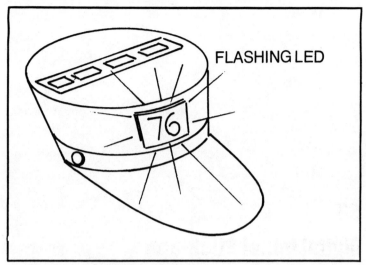

FLASHING LED

Fig. 57-2. Solar powered LED hat in operation.

58
Digital Initial Stick-up

This gadget, when mounted on a door or locker, will tell the rest of the world electronically, that this is where you reside. Wire a pair of digital LEDs to spell your initials and connect them in parallel to mini battery pack and mini switch as shown in Figs. 58-1 and 58-2. Now, mount the parts on a piece of triangular cardboard. Cover the cardboard with dark translucent plastic. You can attach small "stick on adhesive squares" to the back of the reminder or small magnets, whichever will be more useful. Position the LED reminder on a door and it will, when turned on, beacon your presence. See Fig. 58-3.

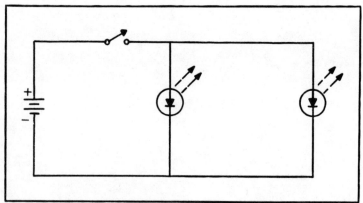

Fig. 58-1. Digital initial stick-up schematic.

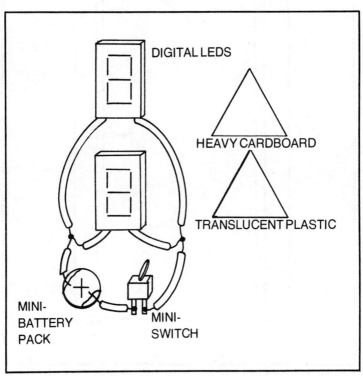

Fig. 58-2. Digital initial wiring diagram.

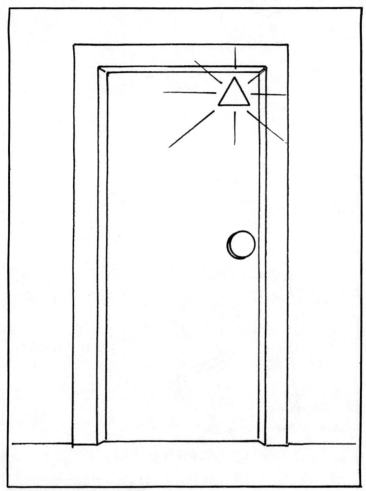

Fig. 58-3. Initial stick-up in use.

59
LED Book Reminder

You can remind yourself of important reading assignments with this easy to build gadget. Wire two flasher LEDs in parallel to a mini battery pack and a mercury switch. See Figs. 59-1 and 59-2. Now, write a motivating message on the front of a piece of heavy cardboard and cover it with protective plastic. Punch small holes in the cardboard for the LED's light to emit through and secure the mini circuit to the back of the message reminder. Position the LEDs so they will shine through the small holes. See Fig. 59-3.

Whenever you want to remind yourself of a reading assignment put this electronic book reminder in the book and place the book flat on a table top. The mercury switch will turn on the circuit and the LEDs will catch your eye if you are in the room. To turn the device off, simply turn it over.

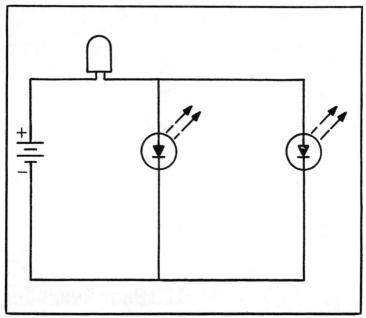

Fig. 59-1. LED book reminder schematic.

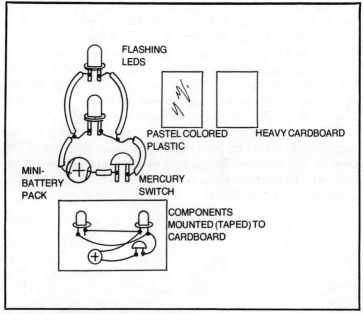

Fig. 59-2. LED book reminder wiring diagram.

Fig. 59-3. Book message reminder in operation.

60
General Purpose Reminder Device

This device can be placed on or in so many places that it's only fitting description is "general purpose". Wire a flashing LED in series with a mini-battery pack and a normally closed (NC) switch. Write down your desired message with a marking pen on a piece of translucent, pastel colored plastic. See Fig. 60-1. Tape the components to a piece of heavy cardboard and tape the plastic over the components. See Fig. 60-2. Depending upon the message and usage, the device has unlimited uses. You can put it in a closet, drawer, cabinet, office or kitchen. Position the NC switch so it rests on something when off, (door or wall, etc.). See Fig. 60-3.

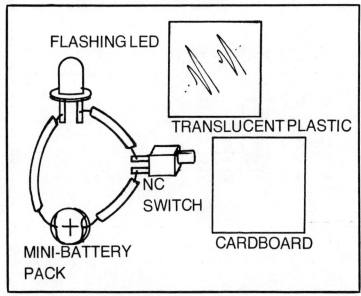

FLASHING LED

TRANSLUCENT PLASTIC

NC
SWITCH

CARDBOARD

MINI-BATTERY
PACK

Fig. 60-1. Reminder wiring diagram.

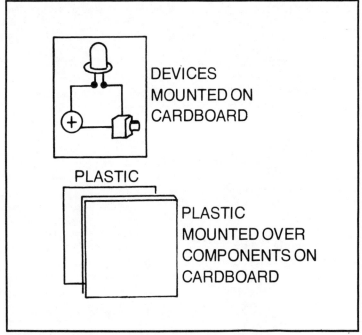

DEVICES
MOUNTED ON
CARDBOARD

PLASTIC

PLASTIC
MOUNTED OVER
COMPONENTS ON
CARDBOARD

Fig. 60-2. Finishing the reminder.

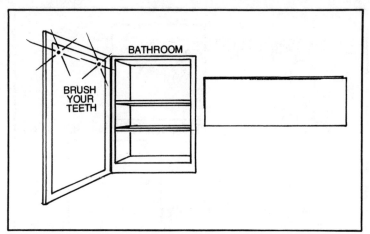

Fig. 60-3. Using the reminder.

61
Vest

If you want to be very flashy at your next party, then construct this novel vest project. Obtain a vest that meets your style and color preferences and attach various LEDs (digital, multicolored, flasher) to it in different places. Wire the LEDs in series to mercury switches and use long wire leads as the mercury switches will be placed on the cuff part of a mini bracelet. See Figs. 61-1 and 61-2.

Tape all of the mercury switch leads together with plastic electrical tape and position and secure the mercury switches to a wristband or bracelet as shown in Fig. 61-3.

Now as you dance and move your arms around the LEDs will light up in different eye appealing patterns. See Fig. 61-4.

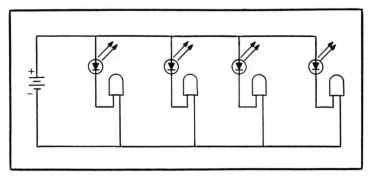

Fig. 61-1. Vest schematic.

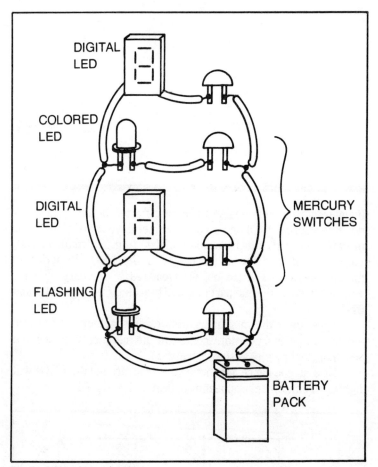

Fig. 61-2. Vest wiring diagram.

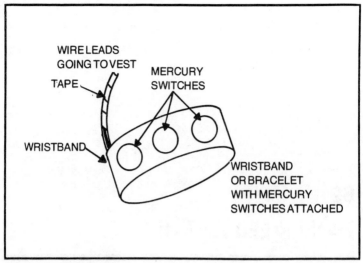

Fig. 61-3. Vest wristband.

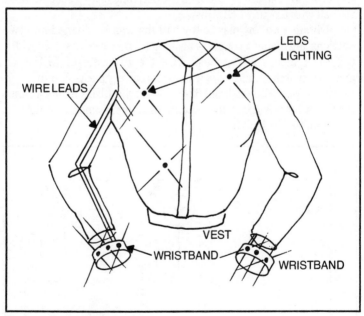

Fig. 61-4. The completed project!

62

Flashing LED Toy Ball

Here'a a gift that will brighten up the playtime of a young one. It's a toy ball with flashing LEDs inside.

Obtain a hollow plastic toy ball that can be divided into two sections and mount a couple of flashing LEDs wired in series with a couple of mercury switches. Wire the two sets of LEDs and mercury switches in parallel with a mini battery pack—2 thin watch batteries. See Fig. 62-1 and 62-2. Mount the LEDs firmly against the ball's inner surface to allow the maximum amount of light to emanate. See Fig. 62-3.

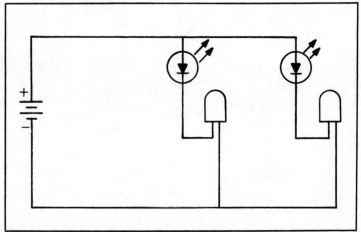

Fig. 62-1. Flashing toy ball schematic.

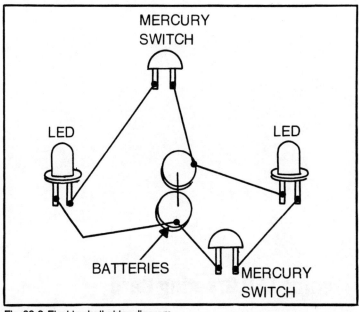

Fig. 62-2. Flashing ball wiring diagram.

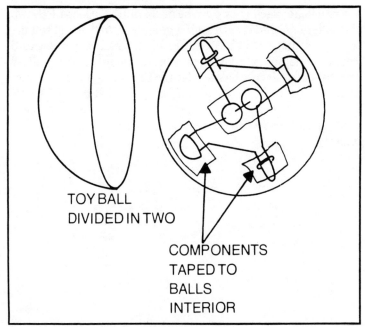

Fig. 62-3. Finishing the flashing toy ball.

63
Flashing LED Greeting Card

A very unique greeting card can be made with a flashing LED, two thin batteries wired in series and a greeting card that will suit the taste of its intended owner. See Fig. 63-1. Obtain a greeting card that has a multiple ply cover since the components will be fitted between two of the plies. Assemble the LED mini-circuit. See Fig. 63-2. Insert the circuit in the card's cover so that the LEDs light will emit from an appropriate area on the cover. See Fig. 63-3. Make small holes in the cover so the light can shine through properly.

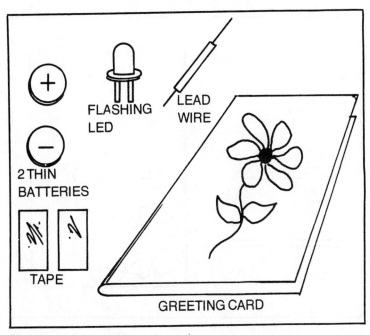

Fig. 63-1. Parts for the LED greeting card.

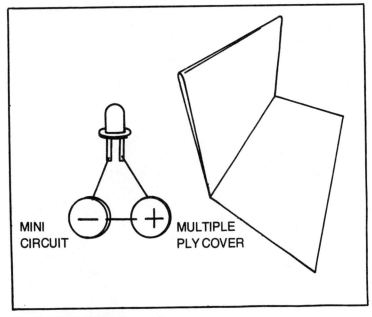

Fig. 63-2. The LED circuit.

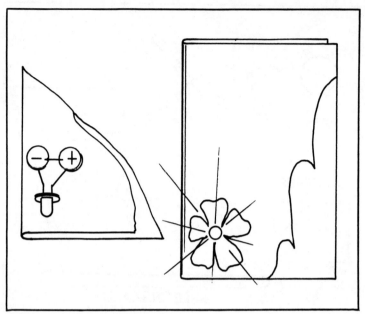

Fig. 63-3. Flashing LED greeting card in use.

64

Position Sensitive LED Greeting Card

You can increase the novelty and the battery life of the greeting card by wiring a miniature mercury switch in series with the circuit. See Fig. 64-1. Simply wire the mercury switch in series with the LED greeting card circuit, shown in Project 63 and position it so the LED will flash when the card is held upright. See Fig. 64-2.

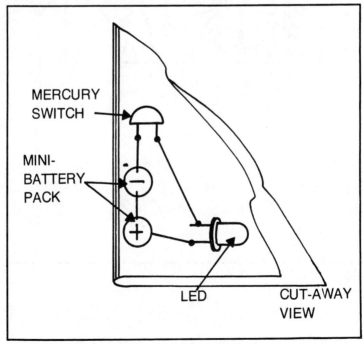

Fig. 64-1. Wiring the position sensitive LED greeting card.

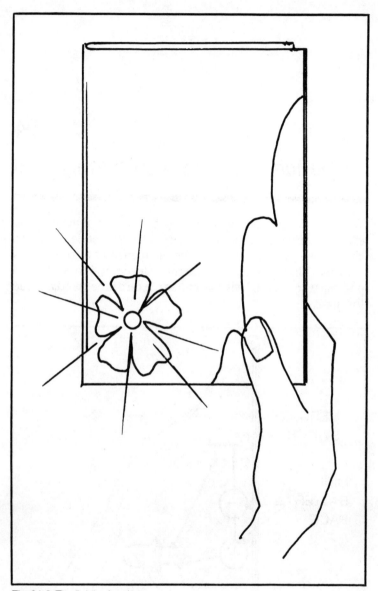

Fig. 64-2. The finished project.

65

Magnetically
Sensitive LED Greeting Card

If you add a reed switch circuit, a greeting card will light when a magnet is placed near it.

Wire the reed switch in series with the LED and mini-battery pack and position it near the lower portion of the card. See Fig. 65-1. To make the effect interesting, glue a small magnet to a ring. You can now control the card's LED with your ring (a perfect excuse for you to make frequent visits). See Fig. 65-2.

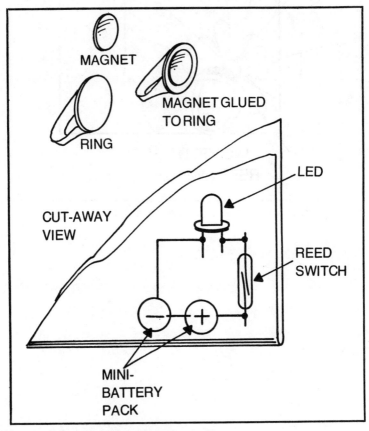

Fig. 65-1. Wiring the reed switch into the circuit.

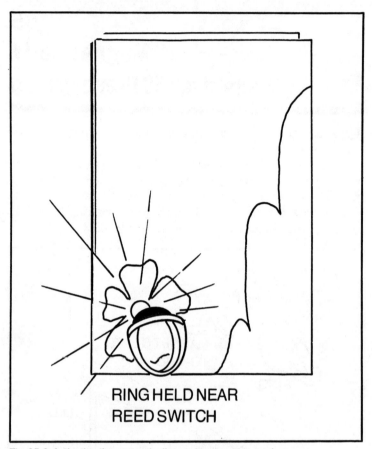

RING HELD NEAR
REED SWITCH

Fig. 65-2. Activating the magnetically sensitive greeting card.

66
Two-Color LED Greeting Card

By substituting a tri-colored LED (it produces two different colors depending on the polarity of power going into it) and adding another set' mercury switch and mini-battery pack, you can produce another variation of the LED greeting card. This one will produce two different colors from the same LED, depending upon which position the card is in.

Construction is similar to the LED greeting card project with the addition of a parallel circuit (mercury switch, mini-battery pack) that is wired in reverse polarity. See Fig. 66-1.

There are many ways you can use the changing colors on the card to add a very special personal touch. See Fig. 66-2.

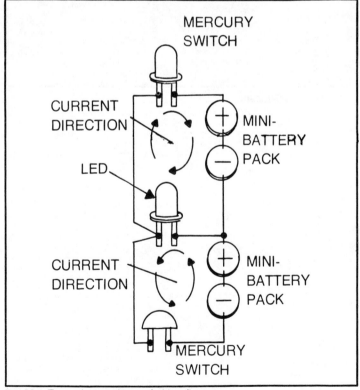

Fig. 66-1. Two-color greeting card wiring diagram.

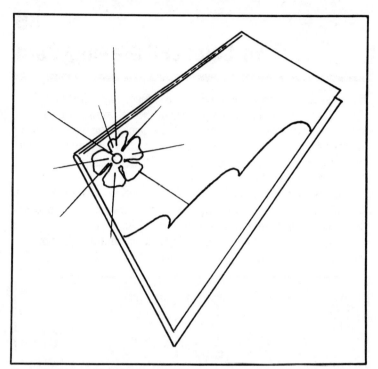

Fig. 66-2. The finished card.

LEDs can be arranged in all sorts of variations on all types of hats. Wire a LED in series with a mini-switch and mini-battery pack. See Fig. 67-1. You might want to add a mercury switch in series with the circuit so the LED will light in accordance to head movements. See Fig. 67-2.

Sew the components securely to a piece of material or a patch, and also sew small snaps to the patch. See Fig. 67-3. In this manner, the component parts can be easily removed when you do not want the hat to flash or if you just want to clean the hat. See Fig. 67-4.

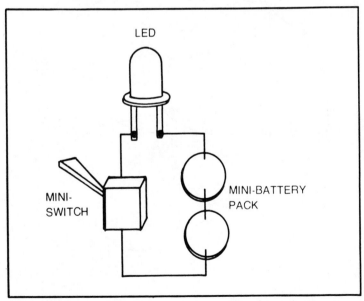

Fig. 67-1. Simple LED circuit.

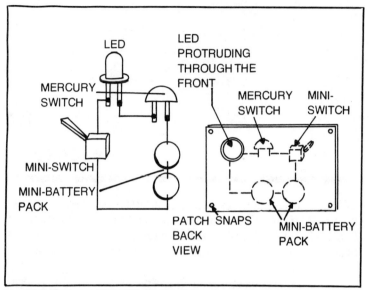

Fig. 67-2. Mercury switch added to circuit.

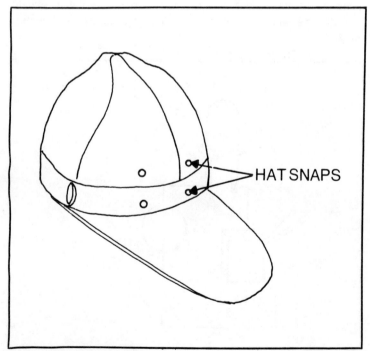

Fig. 67-3. Attaching the snaps.

180

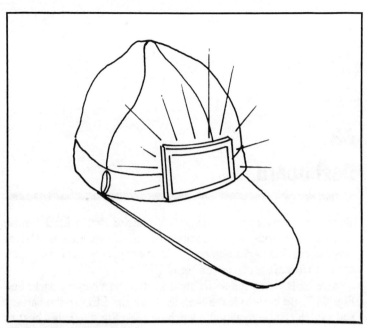

Fig. 67-4. The finished project.

68
Dashboard

There are many places in an auto's interior that a LED can be mounted to serve as a reminder or as an ornamental device. Dashboards, doors, headliners, instrument panels and floorboards are just a few of the places to affix a LED.

Wire LEDs in series with a mini-switch and a battery pack. See Fig. 68-1. Be sure to leave long leads for the LED so the battery and switch can be mounted elsewhere. See Fig. 68-2. It's best to use a separate power supply (battery pack) for the LEDs instead of wiring them to the car's battery.

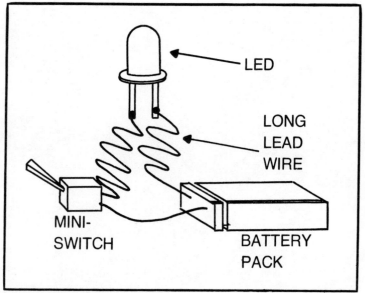

Fig. 68-1. Dashboard wiring diagram.

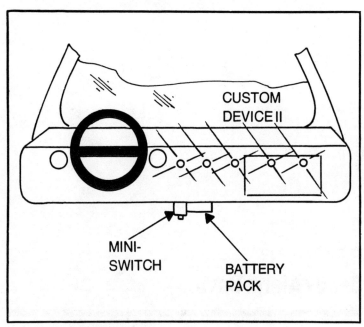

Fig. 68-2. The finished dashboard.

69
Decoy Alarm Device

There are many auto theft systems employed on cars that have a small LED on the fender warning that the system is in operation. You can install this simple, economical device on your auto and have the same "psychological protection."

Construct a circuit consisting of a LED, a battery pack and a mini-switch. See Fig. 69-1. Drill a small hole in the car's fender and mount the LED there. Feed the wires into the interior compartment to the mini-switch and battery pack mounted under the dash. See Fig. 69-2.

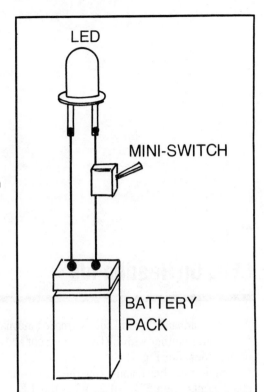

LED

MINI-SWITCH

Fig. 69-1. Decoy alarm
wiring diagram.

BATTERY
PACK

Fig. 69-2. Decoy alarm in use.

70
LEDs On Headbands

A novel headband that will surely amaze (and maybe amuse) friends can be put together with LEDs on the front and a mini-battery pack on the sides. See Fig. 70-1.

Sew two headbands together to form a pocket for the components. See Fig. 70-2. Wire the LEDs in parallel with a mini-switch and a mini-battery pack. Arrange the parts so they will distribute the weight evenly and not bulge. Make small holes in the second headband to let light emanate. See Fig. 70-3.

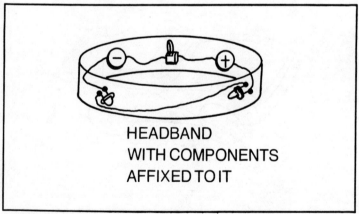

HEADBAND
WITH COMPONENTS
AFFIXED TO IT

Fig. 70-1. Mounting the LEDs on a headband.

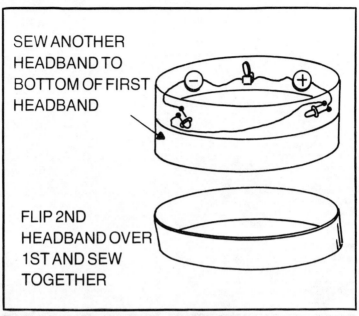

SEW ANOTHER HEADBAND TO BOTTOM OF FIRST HEADBAND

FLIP 2ND HEADBAND OVER 1ST AND SEW TOGETHER

Fig. 70-2. Attaching a second headband over the first.

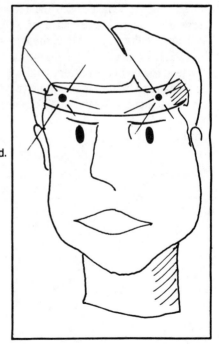

Fig. 70-3. The finished headband.

71
Ring

A neat ring can be made with just a few parts. Find a ring with a big
surface and a removable ornament. Affix a mini-battery pack on the
back area of the ring and lead the wires to the face of the ring. See
Fig. 71-1. Mount the LED on the surface of the ring and connect
one lead to one of the battery leads. See Fig. 71-2. The remaining
LED lead and battery lead will be twisted together when you want
the ring to light. Affix the ring's ornament to the ring's surface area
and position it so it will conceal the LED and also let light shine
through.

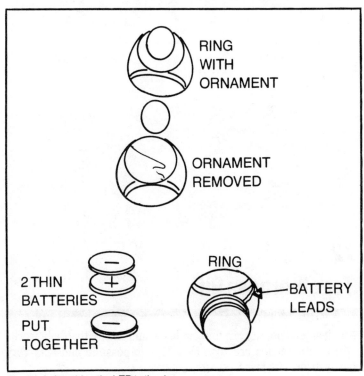

RING
WITH
ORNAMENT

ORNAMENT
REMOVED

2 THIN
BATTERIES

PUT
TOGETHER

RING

BATTERY
LEADS

Fig. 71-1. Attaching the LED to the ring.

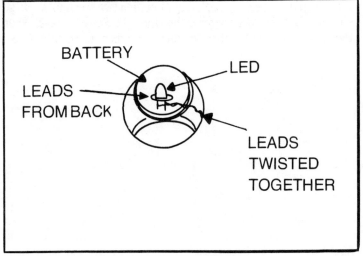

BATTERY

LED

LEADS
FROM BACK

LEADS
TWISTED
TOGETHER

Fig. 71-2. Wiring the LED to the mini-battery pack.

72
Togetherness Gift

An ideal (and poetic) gift for couples would be one that only works when both parties are together. This is possible and also very easily made with just a few simple parts.

Wire two sets of LEDs, reed switches and mini-battery packs in series. See Fig. 72-1. Position them in two identical gifts with room inside for these components. Position two small magnets so each will face the reed switch in the other gift. See Fig. 72-2. When the gifts come together they will turn each other on. See Fig. 72-3.

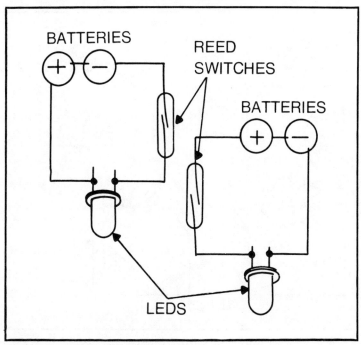

Fig. 72-1. Togetherness gift wiring diagram.

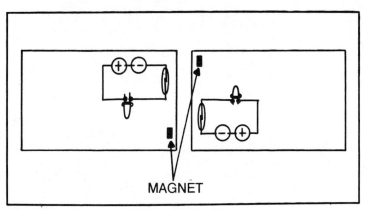

Fig. 72-2. Positioning the magnets and reed switches.

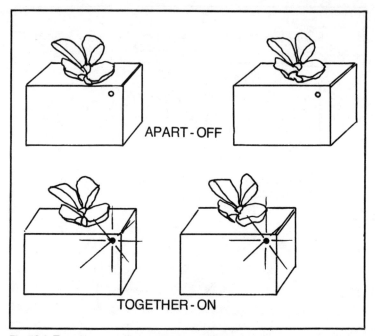

APART - OFF

TOGETHER - ON

Fig. 72-3. Togetherness gifts—turning each other on!

73
Shoes

Yes, even shoes can be turned into lively pieces of attire and entertainment.

You can attach a mini-battery pack, mini-switch and LEDs combo almost anyplace on footwear and the effect will add to any disco, dance, skating or other social event. See Figs. 73-1 and 73-2.

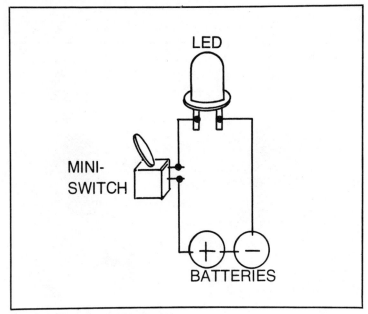

Fig. 73-1. Disco shoes wiring diagram.

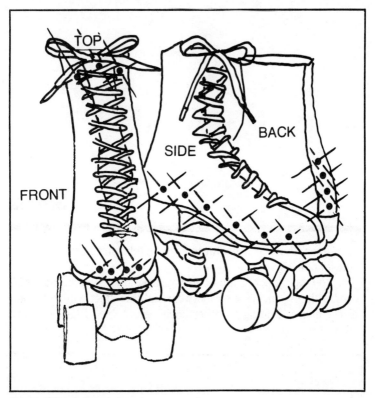

Fig. 73-2. The finished shoes.

74

Shirts And Tops

There have been many disco flashing LED shirts sold but you can add the personal touch and make one for a fraction of the cost of the mass market kinds.

Sew the LEDs onto the back of a piece of material, wired in parallel. Place a small slotted hole in the shirt for the mini-battery pack to go through and be hidden from view. See Figs. 74-1 and 74-2. The piece of material should be colorful and with a picture design of your choice on it.

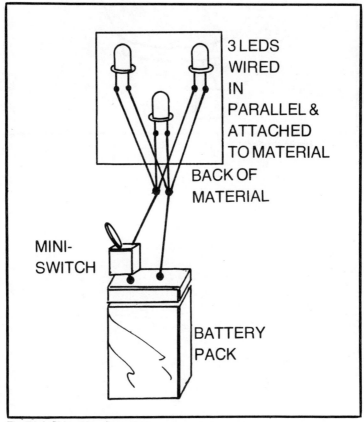

Fig. 74-1. Shirt wiring diagram.

Fig. 74-2. The finished shirt.

75

Flashing LEDs On A Hanging Design

Right in the middle of the room, hanging from the ceiling is a design of unusual shape with blinking lights! Surely this will add excitement and appeal to your next social gathering.

Construct the mini-circuit, three flashing LEDs, mini-switch and a mini-battery pack in series, on a piece of stiff wire or a hanger. See Fig. 75-1. Bend the wire into an unusual shape and tape the components securely. You can decorate this device to your own taste if you wish. See Fig. 75-2.

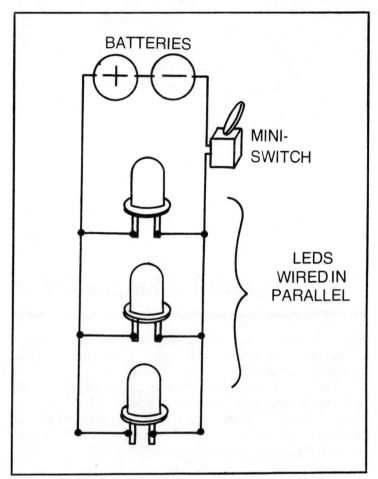

Fig. 75-1. Art design circuit wiring diagram.

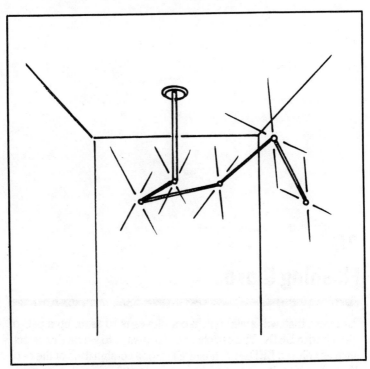

Fig. 75-2. The finished project.

76
Flashing Gloves

An effect that will stand out like a glove, is to team up a pair of
gloves with LEDs. You can choose many ways to set up this effect,
such as colored LEDs, flashing LEDs, or a combination of the two.
Have the circuit controlled by a mini-switch or with a mercury
switch (or two). Figures 76-1 and 76-2 will supply you with a few
examples. Mount components in the wrist area of the glove for
convenience and versatility of hand movement.

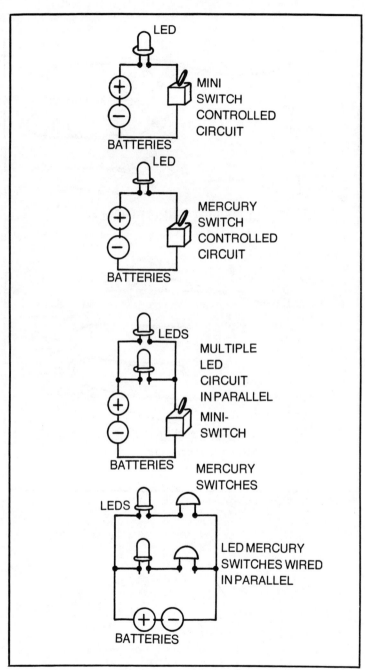

Fig. 76-1. Various ways to wire your flashing gloves.

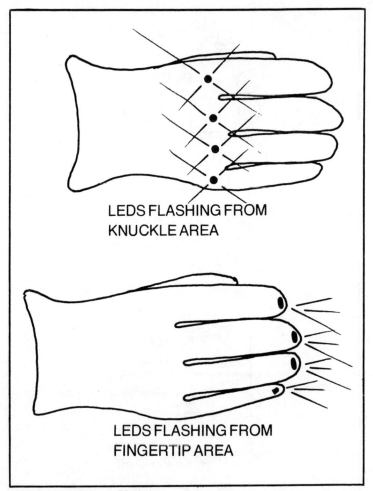

LEDS FLASHING FROM KNUCKLE AREA

LEDS FLASHING FROM FINGERTIP AREA

Fig. 76-2. The finished LED gloves.

77

LED Glasses

Now you can really make a spectacle of yourself . . . with LED glasses.

Obtain a pair of thick framed glasses (preferably shaded) and mount a mini-battery pack, mini-switch and mini-LED or two (flashing or multi-colored) on the inside of the frame in series. Position the mini-LEDs carefully on the front side of the frame. See Figs. 77-1 and 77-2.

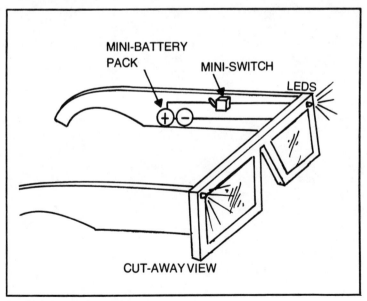

Fig. 77-1. Glasses wiring diagram.

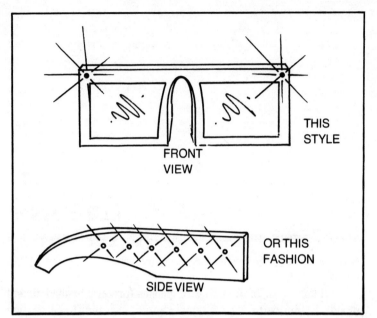

THIS STYLE

FRONT VIEW

OR THIS FASHION

SIDE VIEW

Fig. 77-2. Two different ways to mount the LEDs.

78
Flashing LEDs With Optical Illusions

An unusual conversation piece can be produced very simply and will definitely prove interesting to the eye.

Find a booklet on optical illusions—available at most libraries or bookstores—and sketch an illusion that appeals to you. Reproduce the sketch on a poster board in a neat and artistic fashion and use as much contrast as possible (in colors). Wire three sets of LEDs (flashing) in series with three pots (variable resistors). Wire the LED and pot sets in parallel with each other and connect them to a mini-switch and mini-battery pack. See Fig. 78-1. Set the pots so the flashing LEDs will have a different rate of flash and seem sequential. Place the LEDs behind the optical illusion poster in the appropriate positions and turn your room lights out. See Fig. 78-2.

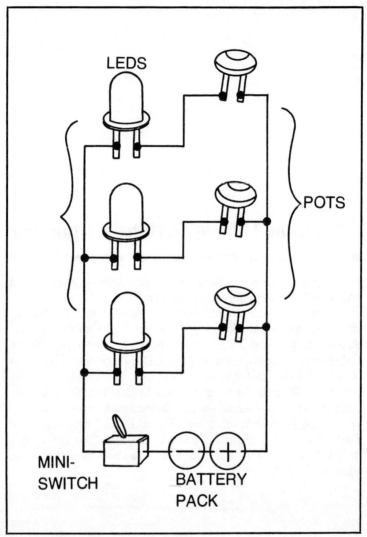

Fig. 78-1. Optical illusion wiring diagram.

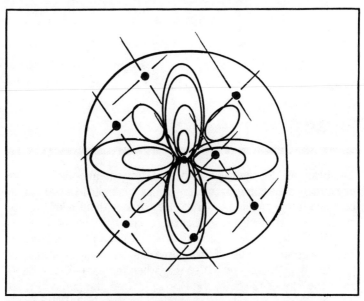

Fig. 78-2. The finished optical illusion poster.

79
Purse Alarm

An ideal gift for females who sometimes leave their purses unguarded is the purse alarm. It is compact, simple to make and can be fitted into a medium to large size purse without taking up too much room. Basically it is a buzzer, battery pack and mercury switch wired in series. See Fig. 79-1. To operate, position the alarm securely in one of the purse's inner compartments and position the mercury switch so that when the purse is laid on its side, the buzzer is off (or vice versa). When the purse is tilted upright, the buzzer will sound loudly. See Fig. 79-2. When not in use, disconnect the battery pack.

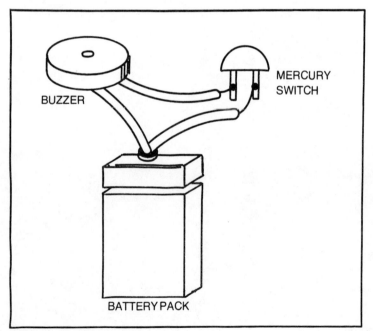

Fig. 79-1. Purse alarm wiring diagram.

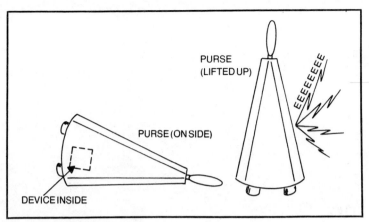

Fig. 79-2. Purse alarm in use.

80
Radio

A nice and simple way to jazz up small radios is accomplished very easily with the aid of a few flashing LEDs. Wire three flashing LEDs in series with the radio's battery (9-volt) and a mercury switch. Make small holes in the radio's case (plastic) and tape the LEDs near the holes on the inside of the radio so light can emanate. See Figs. 80-1 and 80-2. When no in use, tip the radio on it's side to turn off the "light show".

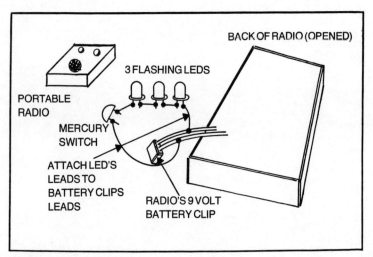

Fig. 80-1. Radio wiring diagram.

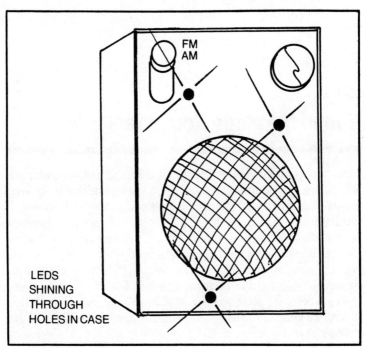

FM
AM

LEDS
SHINING
THROUGH
HOLES IN CASE

Fig. 80-2. Radio in use.

81
Taped Message Reminder

If you've ever wanted to remind yourself or others of something in a way which only your voice could do , then this device is for you. Depending on where you are, or what situation is involved, a normally closed (NC) switch or a mercury switch wired in series with a portable tape recorder can do wonders as a reminding device. If you want a message to be played when you open a door (refrigerator, garage door, etc.) mount a NC switch on the door header so when the door is closed, the switch is off. When it's open, the tape recorder plays a pre-recorded message. See Fig. 81-1. A mercury switch can be used in the same manner if the door is of the swinging type. See Fig. 81-2.

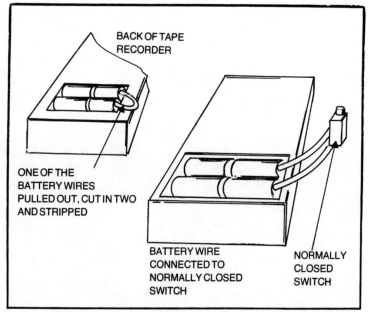

Fig. 81-1. Taped message reminder wiring diagram.

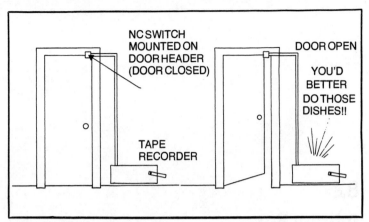

Fig. 81-2. Connecting the door switch.

82
Infinity Box

This device will add intrigue to your next social gathering. It is called an "infinity box" because when you look inside the image seems to go on forever. Obtain some one way mirror paper (the kind used to make auto windows look like one way glass) and some regular reflective paper (available at wallpaper stores) and a small cardboard box, 3 flashing LEDs, a mercury switch and a 9-volt battery and clip.

Cut a round hole in the front of the cardboard box and tape the one way mirror paper so that you can see into the box from the outside. See Fig. 82-1. Tape the reflective paper on the inside back of the box. See Fig. 82-2. Wire the 3 flashing LEDs in series to a mercury switch and the 9-volt battery clip. See Fig. 82-3. Attach the 9-volt battery to its clip and mount the circuit in the box with the LEDs in various positions. Decorate the outside of the box to suit your taste. When the box is tipped upright, the LEDs will flash, as you look into the box through the one way mirror paper you see a multiple reflection of the LEDs flashing in the reflective surfaces of the reflective paper and the reflective side of the one way mirror paper. See Fig. 82-4.

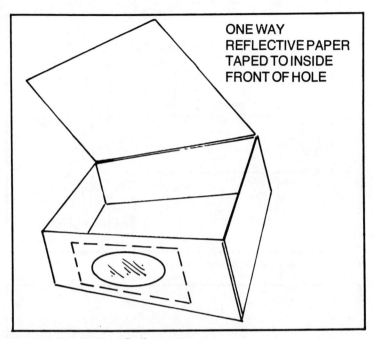

ONE WAY
REFLECTIVE PAPER
TAPED TO INSIDE
FRONT OF HOLE

Fig. 82-1. Attaching the reflective paper.

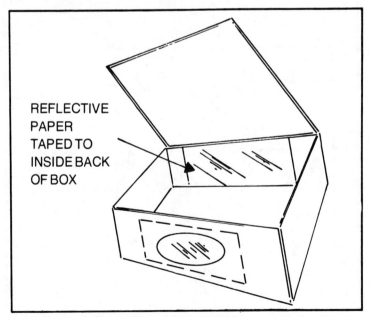

REFLECTIVE
PAPER
TAPED TO
INSIDE BACK
OF BOX

Fig. 82-2. Placing reflective paper in the back of the box.

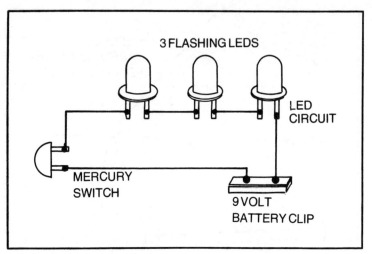

Fig. 82-3. Infinity box wiring diagram.

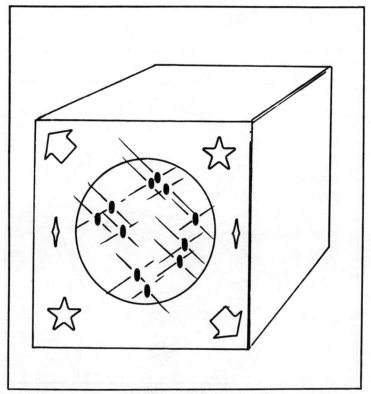

Fig. 82-4. The completed infinity box.

83
Electronic Wand

Many people who frequent discos, roller rinks and the like bring along props such as canes or wands to add to their style of dress or show. You can make a disco wand that will really stand out among your peers in a simple way. Obtain a dowel stick (from a hardware or lumber supply house) and arrange LEDs (regular and flashing) around it. Wire the LEDs in parallel to each other and connect the circuit to a mini-battery pack and switch. See Figs. 83-1 and 83-2. After the circuit is operating and mounted securely, decorate the wand with flashy contact paper with a futuristic pattern. See Fig. 83-3.

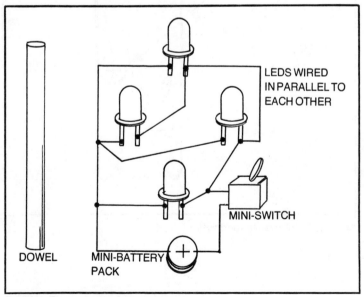

Fig. 83-1. Electronic wand wiring diagram.

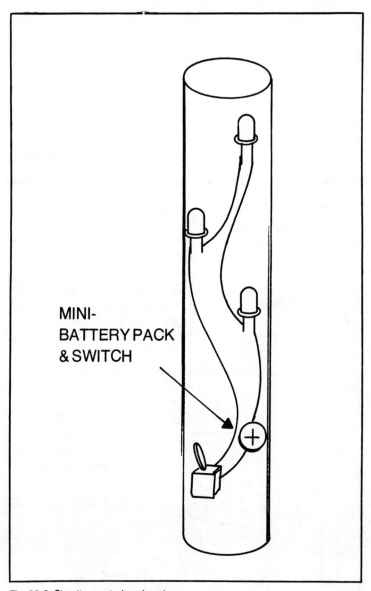

MINI-
BATTERY PACK
& SWITCH

Fig. 83-2. Circuit mounted on dowel.

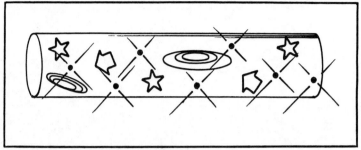

Fig. 83-3. Decorated dowel now becomes wand.

84

Automatic Wand

By adding mercury switches in series with the LEDs on the wand (see Project 83) it will turn on and off automatically when handled. There are many ways to wire this circuit for different effects. If the mercury switches are wired in series with the regular LEDs, then they will alternately flash on and off according to the wands position. This will add to the light show provided by the flashing LEDs. See Fig. 84-1 and 84-2.

With tri-colored LEDs and mercury switches wired in parallel to *two* mini-battery packs, the wand will change colors and seem to flash simultaneously. See Fig. 84-3.

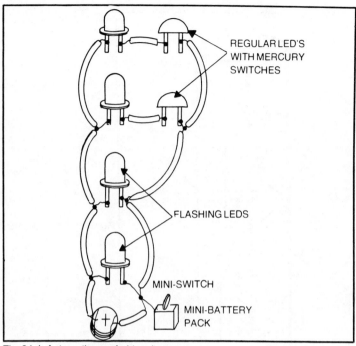

Fig. 84-1. Automatic wand wiring diagram.

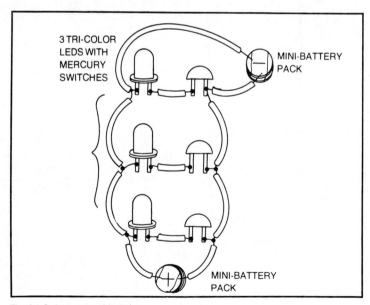

Fig. 84-2. Alternate wiring plan.

221

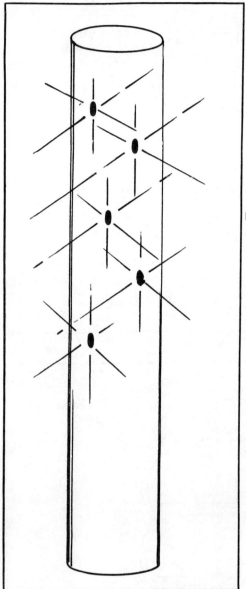

Fig. 84-3. Automatic wand in use.

85
Economical Vanity Mirror

At the last minute you may want to check your appearance before going into a party or social gathering. Here is a neat and economical lighted vanity mirror for your purse or car. Simply wire 4 mini-lights in parallel with a mercury switch and a mini-battery pack. See Fig. 85-1. Position the mercury switch so it will turn on when the mirror is swung down (on a car's sun visor) or tilted up (on a portable purse mirror). See Fig. 85-2.

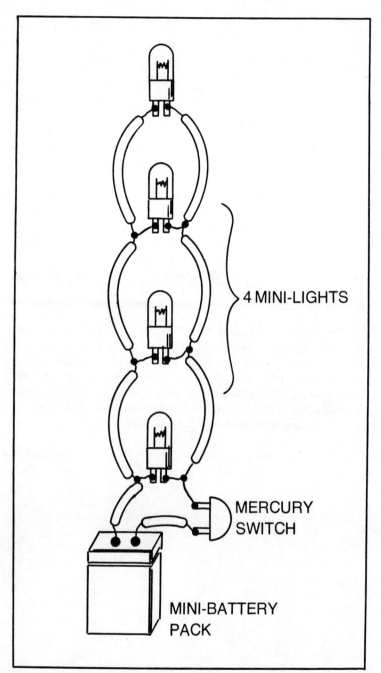

4 MINI-LIGHTS

MERCURY
SWITCH

MINI-BATTERY
PACK

Fig. 85-1. Vanity mirror circuit.

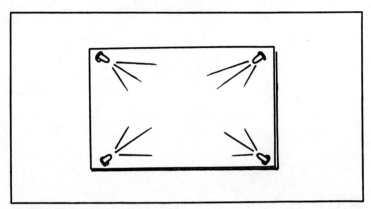

Fig. 85-2. The vanity mirror in operation.

86
Guest Controlled Poster Show

Wire reed switches in series to all of the LEDs in a wall size poster (or LEDs behind wallpaper as seen in Project 3) and you can create a very fascinating addition to any party. Arrange the reed switches to correspond to the positions of the LEDs on the poster. See Figs. 86-1 and 86-2.

Attach elastic straps to some fairly large magnets and have your guests wear them on their palms. As their hands sweep across the control board, the lights will light on the poster in correlation to their hand movement. See Fig. 86-3. Arrange different types of LEDs in the poster for an interesting light display (multi-color, flashing, etc.).

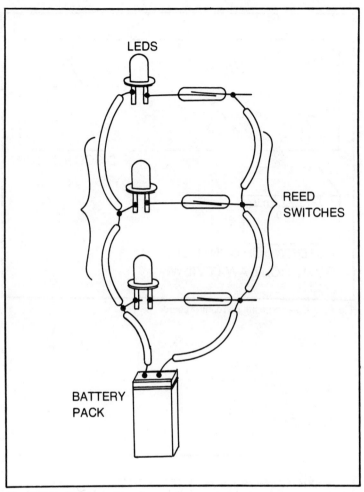

Fig. 86-1. Poster show wiring diagram.

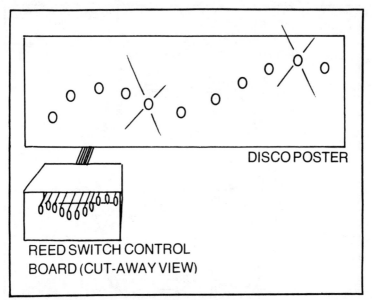

DISCO POSTER

REED SWITCH CONTROL
BOARD (CUT-AWAY VIEW)

Fig. 86-2. Detail of poster and control board.

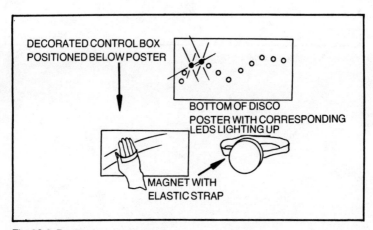

DECORATED CONTROL BOX
POSITIONED BELOW POSTER

BOTTOM OF DISCO
POSTER WITH CORRESPONDING
LEDS LIGHTING UP

MAGNET WITH
ELASTIC STRAP

Fig. 86-3. Poster show in operation.

87
Poster Show With Control Pole

A variation of the previous project the guest controlled poster, can be controlled with a single floor to ceiling pole.

Arrange the reed switches all around the pole and cover the pole entirely with decorative tape. Lead the reed switch's lead wires to the poster and connect them to the individual LEDs on the poster. See Figs. 87-1 and 87-2.

Use a small wristband with magnets attached as the activator for the disco poster. Now your guests can control the poster as they dance and mingle around the dance floor. See Fig. 87-3.

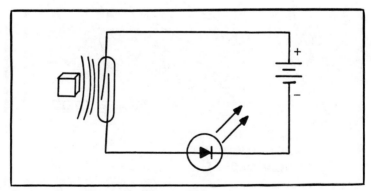

Fig. 87-1. Poster with control pole schematic.

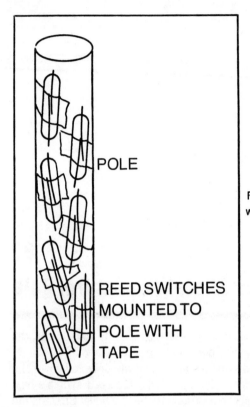

POLE

REED SWITCHES
MOUNTED TO
POLE WITH
TAPE

Fig. 87-2. Covering the pole
with reed switches.

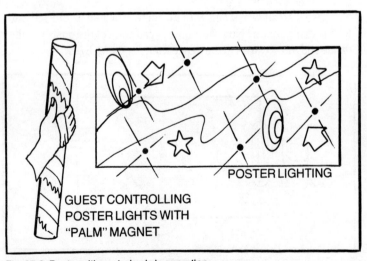

POSTER LIGHTING

GUEST CONTROLLING
POSTER LIGHTS WITH
"PALM" MAGNET

Fig. 87-3. Poster with control pole in operation.

88
Multicolored Poster

You can produce a more colorful light show on your poster (as described in Project 87) by wiring multicolored LEDs to a flasher IC. See Figs. 88-1 and 88-2.

Arrange the LEDs on the poster's backside so their different colors accent the poster's color scheme. See Fig. 88-3.

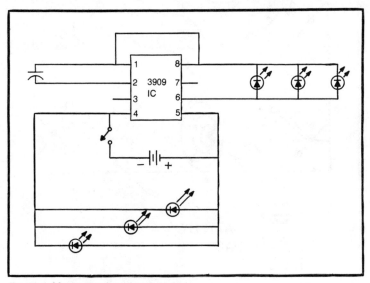

Fig. 88-1. Multicolored poster schematic.

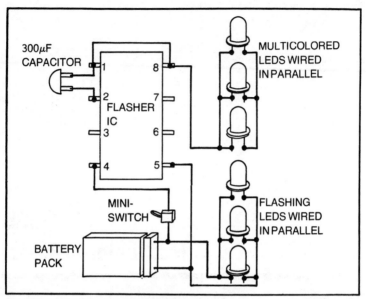

Fig. 88-2. Multicolored poster wiring diagram.

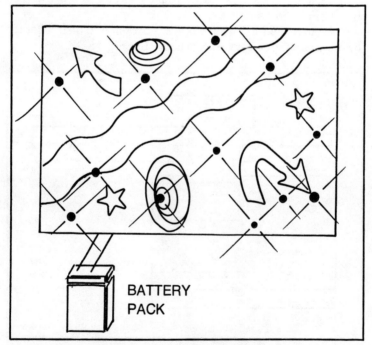

Fig. 88-3. Multicolored flashing LED poster in operation.

232

89
D-J Controlled Light Effects

Here's a simple way to let the D-J of your next party control the room's light show (the disco wall, floor or ceiling posters) along with the music.

Wire a poster so the LEDs will be in series with a switch that is positioned away from the poster with long wire leads. The "switch" will be a piece of cardboard with a group of screw heads protruding from the top. Wire the LED's negative lead to a common wire that is connected to a long bare wire. Wire the LED's positive leads to the different screw heads secured to the cardboard by the screw itself. See Figs. 89-1 and 89-2.

Connect the battery pack in parallel to the LED's and their switches. Now by touching the screw heads with the bare wire, the D-J can have unique control over which lights on the poster go on or off according to the music. See Fig. 89-3.

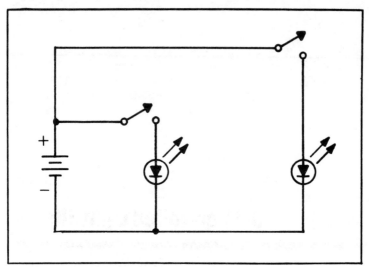

Fig. 89-1. D-J controlled light effects schematic.

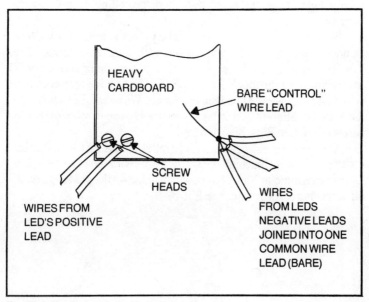

Fig. 89-2. The D-J controlled "switch."

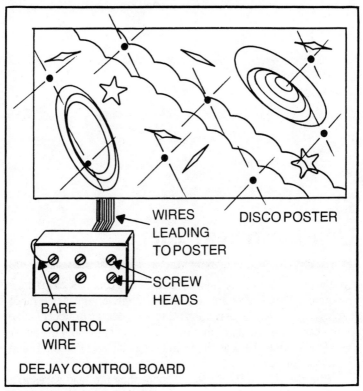

WIRES LEADING TO POSTER

DISCO POSTER

SCREW HEADS

BARE CONTROL WIRE

DEEJAY CONTROL BOARD

Fig. 89-3. The D-J controlled poster.

90
Radio Controlled Poster

If you want to change the lighting effects in a room as you change your mood, then here's an easy way to do it. Mount some disco posters on your den or recreation room wall, ceiling or floor. Leave out the battery packs and substitute the lead wires from the super simple radio control box as shown in Project 25. See Fig. 90-1. You can choose the manner of lighting to reflect your tastes.

With the right combination of connecting the lead wires to a tri-colored LED, the poster will change colors as you press the hand unit's button.

You can have flashing LEDs always on (wired in series or parallel to their own battery pack) and have the RC box connected to mini-lamps in the poster. This gives a bright light display throughout the room when you desire.

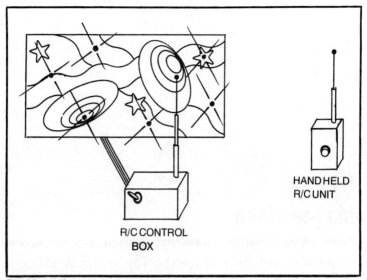

Fig. 90-1. R/C poster.

91
Magne Wand

A nice way to add novelty to a party can be easily accomplished by adding reed switches in series to all of the LEDs on a disco poster. See Fig. 91-1. Obtain some wooden dowels from a hardware store or lumber yard and glue or tape magnets to the tip of the dowel. Decorate the dowels to suit your taste. See Fig. 91-2. Put disco posters on all of the walls in the room and to be really different, on the floors and ceilings. Give the magne disco wands to your guests. Turn on the music, turn down the lights, and watch how they will enjoy "turning on" the posters with their real magic wands! See Fig. 91-3.

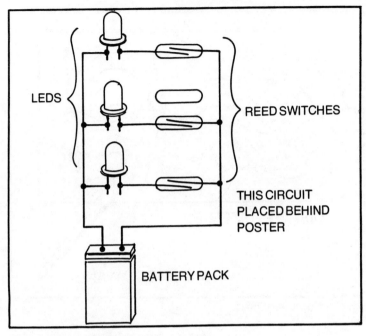

Fig. 91-1. Magne wand operated poster circuit.

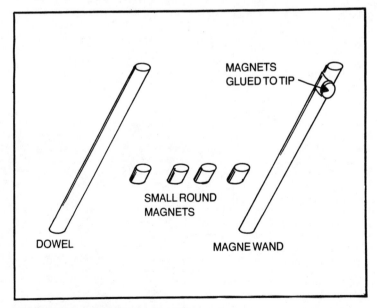

Fig. 91-2. Constructing the magne wand.

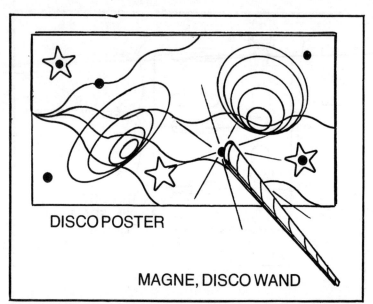

Fig. 91-3. Magne wand in use.

92
Multicolored LED T-Shirt

You can produce a multicolored look on your LED T-shirt (as described in Project 74) with the addition of a flasher IC and capacitor. Simply wire three multicolored LEDs in parallel to the flasher IC and capacitor. Connect the components to a mini-battery pack and a mini-switch. See Figs. 92-1 and 92-2. Attach the component parts to a piece of decorative material cloth and sew this to the front of the T-shirt. Use long lead wire for the mini-switch so it can be placed in your pants pocket. Now, the T-shirt will, when you activate the switch, come to colorful life. See Fig. 92-3.

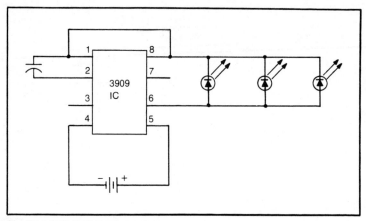

Fig. 92-1. LED T-Shirt schematic.

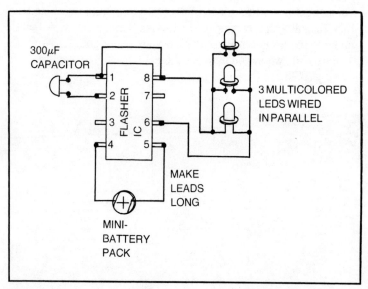

Fig. 92-2. LED T-Shirt wiring diagram.

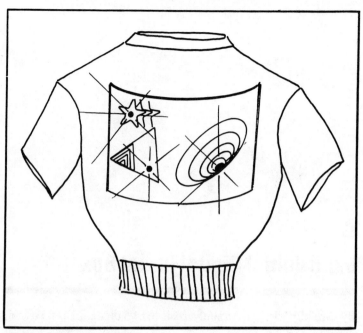

Fig. 92-3. The finished T-Shirt.

93
Multi-Initial Digital Initial Box

By carefully wiring a parallel circuit to two digital LEDs, you can make two sets of initials appear. Wire some of the leads of each LED to its corresponding battery pack and switch to spell out a certain initial. See Figs. 93-1 and 93-2. You can choose several methods of turning on each initial set: mercury switches, reed switches or mini-switches. See Fig. 93-3.

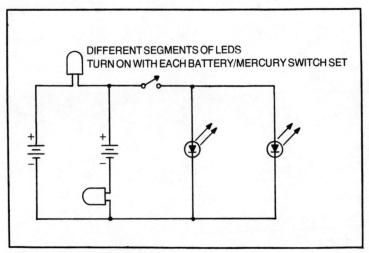

Fig. 93-1. Multi-initial display schematic.

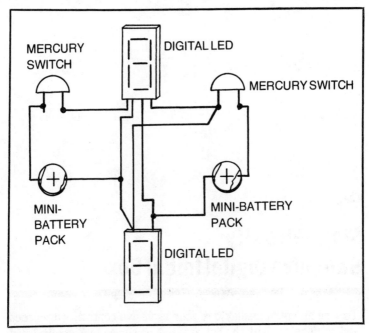

Fig. 93-2. Multi-initial wiring diagram.

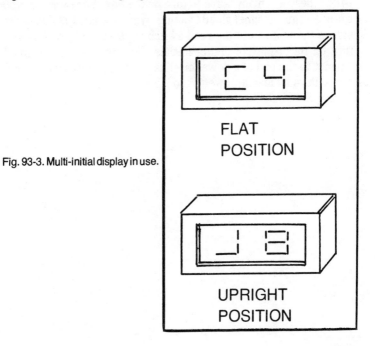

Fig. 93-3. Multi-initial display in use.

FLAT
POSITION

UPRIGHT
POSITION

245

94
Magnetically
Sensitive Digital Initial Box

To give an initial display box your exclusive control, wire a reed switch in series with the battery pack as shown in Figs. 94-1 and 94-2. There are many ways to turn on the box. For example, you can use a small magnet glued to a ring. When you aim the ring at the part of the box where the reed switch is positioned, the box will turn on its display of digital initials. You can also glue a small magnet to the end of a dowel or stick and now control the display box with your "magne power wand". See Fig. 94-3.

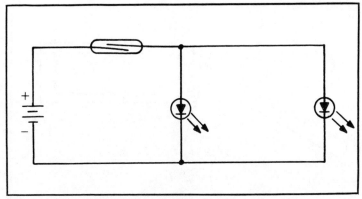

Fig. 94-1. Magnetically sensitive initial box schematic.

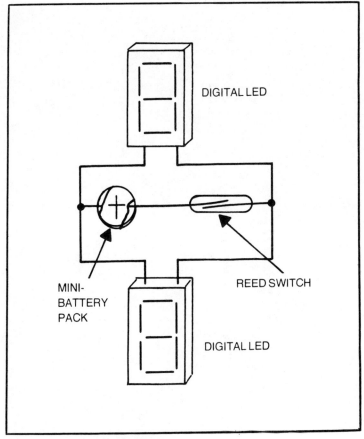

DIGITAL LED

MINI-
BATTERY
PACK

REED SWITCH

DIGITAL LED

Fig. 94-2. Initial box wiring diagram.

247

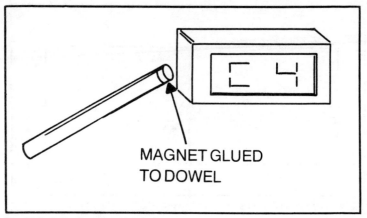

Fig. 94-3. Activating the initial display.

95
Position Sensitive Digital Initial Box

By substituting a mercury switch for a mini-switch, the LED digital initial box will come on automatically when it is positioned upright. See Figs. 95-1 and 95-2. This will also enhance its appearance as there will be no protruding switch showing in the back. See Fig. 95-3.

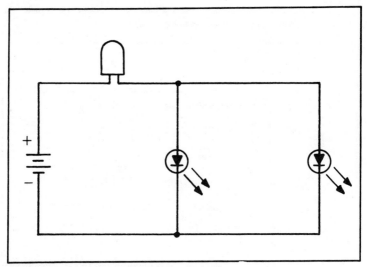

Fig. 95-1. Position sensitive initial box schematic.

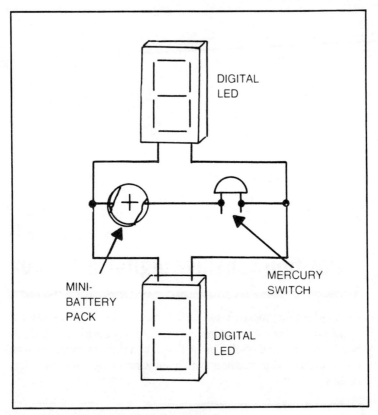

Fig. 95-2. Position sensitive initial box wiring diagram.

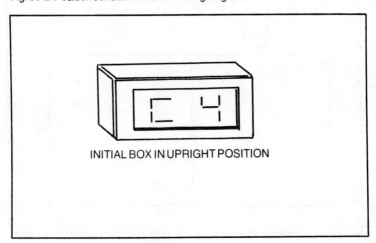

Fig. 95-3. Position sensitive initial box in action.

96
Flashing Digital Initial Bracelet

You can add the "action look" to the digital initial bracelet project described in Project 37 by adding a flasher IC and capacitor. Simply wire the digital LEDs to the flasher IC circuit as shown in Figs. 96-1 and 96-2.

Mount the components on a bracelet and cover the parts with decorative material cloth. See Fig. 96-3.

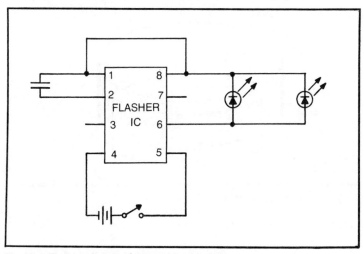

Fig. 96-1. Flashing digital initial bracelet schematic.

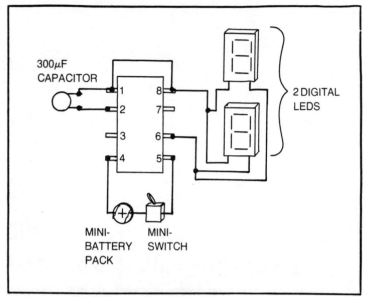

Fig. 96-2. Flashing digital bracelet wiring diagram.

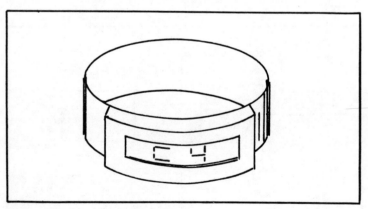

Fig. 96-3. Flashing digital bracelet in use.

97

Dual Message Belt

Here's a variation of the digital message belt that will make it more versatile in operation.

Wire two digital LEDs to spell out a short message (i.e. HI, BY) and wire the LED to spell out another message or your initials by using parallel leads. See Fig. 97-1.

Connect the LED's leads that spell out your initials in series to a mini battery pack and mini switch. See Fig. 97-2.

Now, wire the LED's leads that spell out your other message to a flasher IC with a capacitor, a mini switch and the same mini battery pack.

Package the components neatly on your belt buckle and you can now switch from a flashing message to initials that are on continuously. See Fig. 97-3.

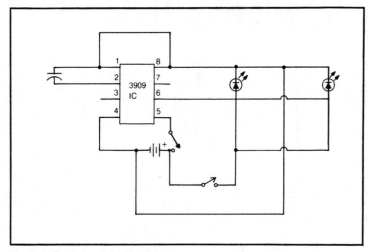

Fig. 97-1. Dual message belt schematic.

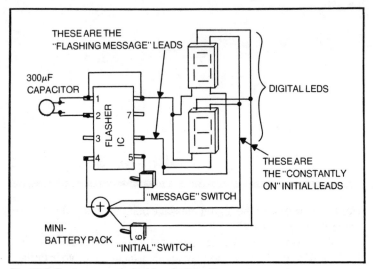

THESE ARE THE
"FLASHING MESSAGE" LEADS

300μF
CAPACITOR

FLASHER IC

DIGITAL LEDS

THESE ARE
THE "CONSTANTLY
ON" INITIAL LEADS

"MESSAGE" SWITCH

MINI-
BATTERY PACK

"INITIAL" SWITCH

Fig. 97-2. Dual message belt wiring diagram.

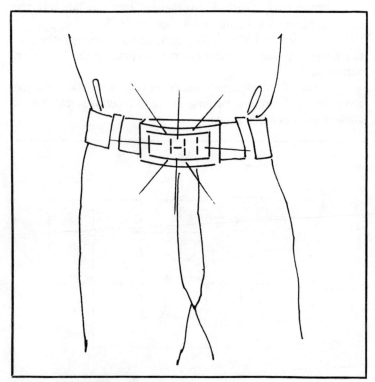

Fig. 97-3. Dual message belt in operation.

254

98

Flashing LED Hood Ornament

You can add a dual function to the LED hood ornament project described in Project 55, by adding a flasher IC, capacitor and another mini-switch to the circuit. Wire the digital LED (spelling out your initial) in series to a mini-battery pack and mini-switch. See Fig. 98-1. Now wire the digital LED in parallel to the flasher IC, capacitor, mini-switch and the same battery pack as shown in Fig. 98-2. Mount the digital LED securely to a hood ornament and mount the ornament on your car's hood. Lead the component parts to the car's interior and mount them under the dash. Mount the mini-switches 1 and 2 on the lower side of the dash so that they can be easily reached. Now, you can make the hood ornament light constantly or flash your initials on and off depending upon which switch you turn on. See Fig. 98-3.

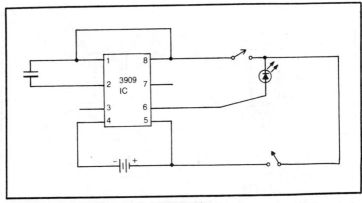

Fig. 98-1. Flashing hood ornament schematic.

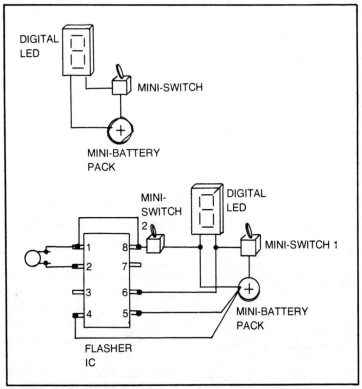

Fig. 98-2. Flashing hood ornament wiring diagram.

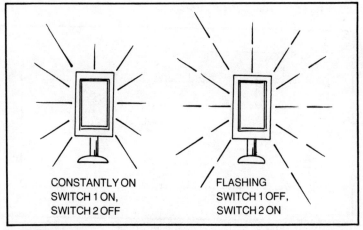

Fig. 98-3. Flashing hood ornament in use.

99

Futuristic Wall Design

You can combine the worlds of futuristic art and disco! You can control the LEDs on a futuristic art poster by using the output of your stereo receiver. Wire the LM3914 bar/dot display IC as shown in Fig. 99-1 to the LEDs on a wall poster. The pot (R2) will adjust the LEDs to respond to the audio output of the music system. Now, the LEDs will "rise and fall" to the sounds of your disco sound system. See Fig. 99-2.

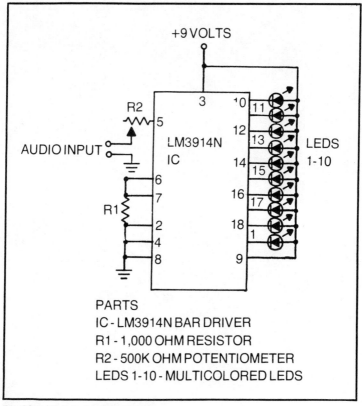

Fig. 99-1. Wall design schematic.

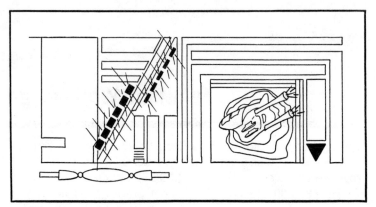

Fig. 99-2. Wall design in operation.

Section III

Bonus Projects

100
IC Controlled Futuristic Wall Design

By adding a 4017 decade counter circuit to the futuristic wall design's LED (see Project 35) they will flash in a sequential pattern. You might also want to connect the output pins to a digital display LED in parallel. Wire the segments of the digital LED to flash some unusual looking displays. Figs. 100-1 and 100-2.

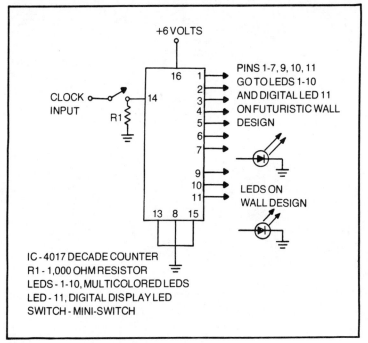

Fig. 100-1. IC controlled wall design schematic.

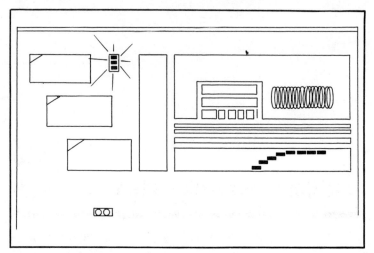

Fig. 100-2. Wall design with decade counter circuit.

101
LED Space Gun With Sound Effects

By adding a small buzzer (wired in parallel to the LED) to the space gun as described in Project 9 you can add the synchronized effect of sound which will really liven up this unique toy. See Figs. 101-1 and 101-2.

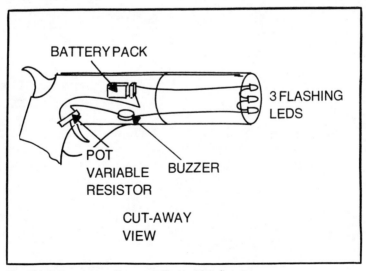

Fig. 101-1. Space gun with sound effects wiring diagrams.

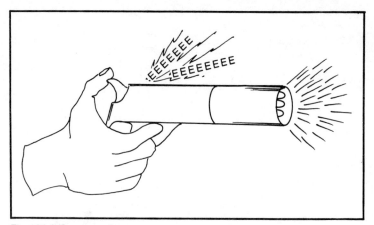

Fig. 101-2. Space gun in use.

102
Solar Powered Initial Box

By substituting four solar cells for the mini-battery pack, your flashing digital initial box will never need battery replacement.

Assemble the flashing initial box as described in Project 2 and wire the four, 1½ volt solar cells in series and connect them to the flasher IC's battery connections (leads 4 and 5). See Figs. 102-1 and 102-2. Now, assemble the box and place the solar cells on the top of the box and it will automatically turn on when in the presence of room light. See Fig. 102-3.

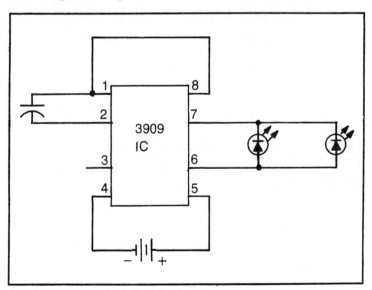

Fig. 102-1. Solar powered initial box schematic.

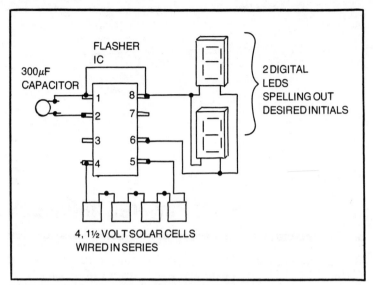

Fig. 102-2. Solar powered initial box wiring diagram.

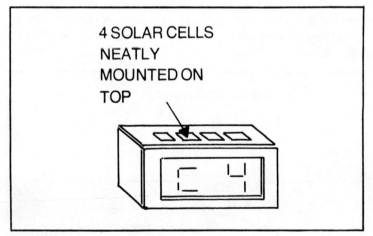

Fig. 102-3. Solar powered initial box in use.

103
Flashing Digital Initial Display

You can add the action effect to your digital initial box by adding a flasher IC to the circuit. Wire the two digital LEDs to spell out your initials and connect them in parallel to the flasher IC and capacitor. Attach the mini-battery pack and the switch of your choice to the IC circuit. See Figs. 103-1 and 103-2.

Package the circuit in a display box with a display window for the LED's light to emit through and cover the window with dark translucent plastic for a blacked out appearance when off. See Fig. 103-3.

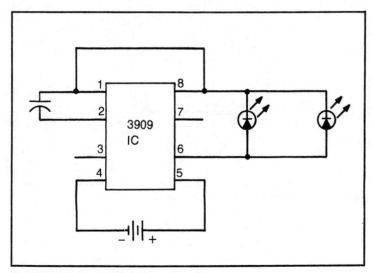

Fig. 103-1. Flashing initial display schematic.

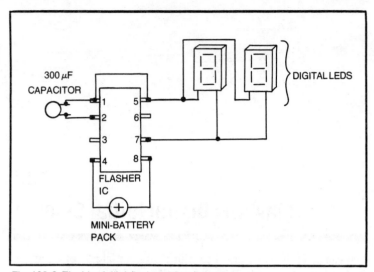

Fig. 103-2. Flashing initial display wiring diagram.

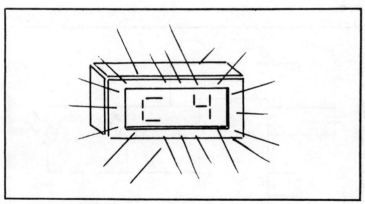

Fig. 103-3. Flashing digital initial box in operation.

104
Ten Extra Bonus Mini-Circuits

The following mini circuits are given to show how easy it is to produce endless combinations of projects by mixing and matching electronic components to control one another and produce various effects.

Touch Switch and Flip-Flop. Can be used in bracelets, pendants, etc. Lets the owner touch the bracelet momentarily to turn it on and view the display and then later touch it again to turn it completely off. See Fig. 104-1.

Touch Switch, Flip-Flop and Delay Off Circuit. Used in jewelry when a "fade away" light display is desired. See Fig. 104-2.

Touch Switch, Flip-Flop and Delay On Circuit. Can be made to produce a message that comes on gradually, and gives a mysterious effect. See Fig. 104-3.

Mercury Switch and Flip-Flop. Just flick your wrist and your bracelet stays on. Flick it again and it goes off. See Fig. 104-4.

Mercury Switch, Flip-Flop and Delay On. When your wrist is in a certain position, the bracelet will gradually come on in an eye appealing manner. See Fig. 104-5.

Mercury Switch, Flip-Flop and Delay Off. When your already on bracelet is flicked again, its display fades away. See Fig. 104-6.

Auto Digital Initial Display with Slow Flash Rate/Fast Flash Rate. Wire a flasher LED in series to your digital LEDs and mount the flasher LED where it will have the car's floor courtesy

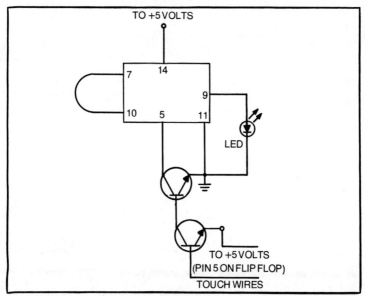

Fig. 104-1. Touch switch and flip-flop circuit.

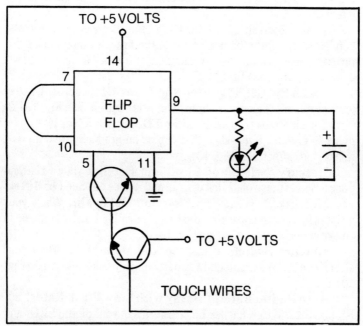

Fig. 104-2. Touch switch, flip-flop and delay off circuit.

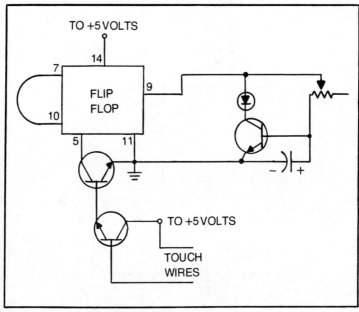

Fig. 104-3. Touch switch flip-flop and delay on circuit.

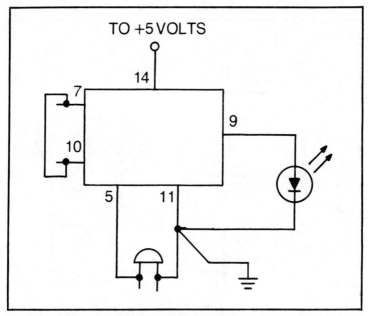

Fig. 104-4. Mercury switch and flip-flop circuit.

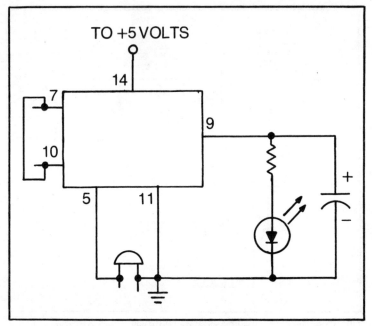

Fig. 104-5. Mercury switch, flip-flop and delay on circuit.

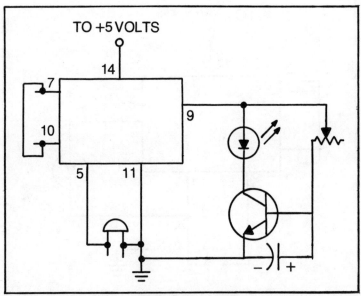

Fig. 104-6. Mercury switch, flip-flop and delay off circuit.

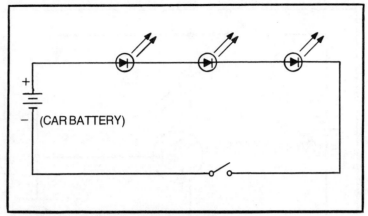

Fig. 104-7. Slow flash and fast flash rate circuit.

lights or dome light shine on it when the door is opened. Now your initials will have a very slow flash rate normally but when the door(s) opens, its rate flashes at about ten times normal speed. See Fig. 104-7.

Door Ajar Initials with Delay Off. Now your digital initial display will stay on for awhile after you turn off the vehicle and depart. See Fig. 104-8.

Digital Initial Display with Delay On. Wired to your ignition switch or light switch, the digital initials will take awhile to come on completely. Looks even better if each initial has its own

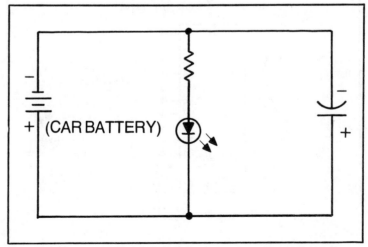

Fig. 104-8. Door ajar with delay off circuit.

273

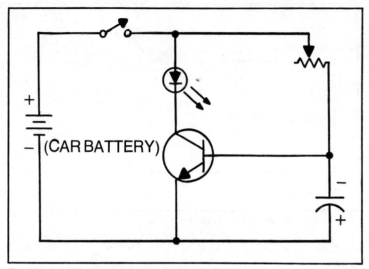

Fig. 104-9. Initial display with delay on circuit.

delay on circuit but with different size capacitors so they come on at different times. See Fig. 104-9.

Auto Dash Message Display Panel. The most elaborate mini-circuit has the best effect. A 555 timer and 4017 decade counter circuit is wired to slowly flash messages to the passenger

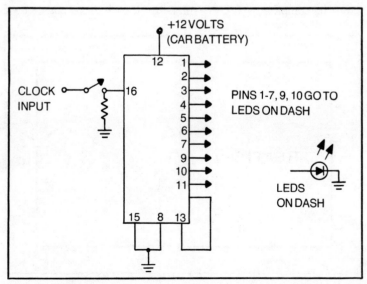

Fig. 104-10. Message display circuit.

of the car. This is done by placing LEDs behind a cardboard cut-out stencil that displays messages like; WELCOME ABOARD, BUCKLE UP, ENJOY THE RIDE and then the owners initials. The initial display will then stay on because a jumper wire is connected from pin 13 of the decade counter IC to the pin that sends power to the LED(s) that display the initials. Of course, as in previous projects of this sort, the LEDs and the cardboard cut-out display are covered with material cloth for a neat appearance. See Fig. 104-10.

I hope you have learned that you can go much further and invent your own combinations of novel circuits with the components used in this book as well as parts found elsewhere.

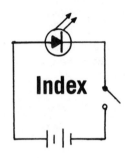

Index

276